Cricket: Styles and Stylists

John Parker

CRICKET
Styles & Stylists

Angus & Robertson · Publishers

Angus & Robertson · Publishers
London · Sydney · Melbourne · Singapore · Manila

First published by Angus and Robertson (UK) Ltd, in 1979

Copyright © John Parker, 1979

ISBN 0 207 95803 3

Typeset in VIP Plantin by Trident Graphics Limited, Reigate, Surrey
Printed in the United Kingdom by W. & J. Mackay Ltd, Chatham

Contents

Introduction

During the preparation of this book, I asked Colin Cowdrey, himself acknowledged as being probably one of the most stylish batsman of his or any other generation, the question that evokes wide-ranging discussion and argument wherever cricketers foregather: "Who do you think was – or is – the most stylish batsman of your time? And why?"

His reply was instant and unequivocal.

"Tom Graveney," he said. 'He began with the advantage of his physique. He was tall and elegant, and so sure in the execution of all his strokes. What's more, he had the ability not only to enjoy making his strokes – the cover-drive wide of the fielder's hand, the perfectly timed on-drive, the clip off the toes – but to communicate that enjoyment. It wasn't done with flourishes; Tom took pleasure in batting well – he *enjoyed* every minute of it.

"But it goes deeper than mannerisms. Graveney was like Walter Hammond before him – every inch the cricketer. When he came down the pavilion steps it was like a guardsman going into battle – everything prepared down to the last detail. His boots would be clean, his bat immaculate, his cap adjusted correctly. He just looked the part, and he stood tall and elegant in his personal life too. Even his handwriting showed the character and style of the man.

"Bowlers? With the fast men it's their rhythm that gives them style. I'd pick Ray Lindwall above them all; he always sought rhythm, pace and accuracy, and he attained them better than any other bowler; of Englishmen, probably Brian Statham came the closest to my definition of style. But of the spinners, when Sonny Ramadhin was weaving his spells in the early 'fifties for West Indies there was no-one to touch him. He was never easy to read, and he could keep going all day long."

Of all the wicketkeepers he had played with and against Cowdrey predictably nominated Godfrey Evans, for his own aggressive style.

"Even when he walked down the wicket between the overs you had to notice him. He projected confidence and swept along all the other members of his team with him. If he dropped a word to the skipper in passing you always felt that he'd hatched a dark and deep new plot to winkle the batsman out, when all he was probably doing was passing the time of day or wondering what beer they served in the pub."

Tom Graveney – every inch a stylist.

The acknowledged greatest batsman of the century, Sir Donald Bradman, wrote to me: "I never considered myself a stylist." A modest assessment which I should think might be challenged by quite a few English bowlers; but he dropped the names of Trumper and McCabe, and The Don's opinion is, as ever in cricket matters, invaluable.

And finally, "Lord Ted" Dexter, whose nickname denotes the style of the man, is in no doubt when it comes to assessing the abilities of the men against whom he has played. His choices, spelled out in his

Cricket Book, are perhaps surprising; they are none the less valid.

"The best bowler I have ever faced – Les Jackson of Derbyshire.

. . . "I walked quite confidently to the middle. No two balls did the same thing, and hardly a straight one was bowled. They bent one way in the air and broke back off the wicket as though controlled on a string. I decided that the one way to survive was to play only to keep my wicket intact, and hope to tire the great man out. I let them hit me on the pads when just outside leg stump, and let them go by within inches of the off stump. Jackson soon banged one down and as I saw it hit the wicket short and a foot outside the off stump, I shouldered arms expecting to see it fly harmlessly by. The next moment I dropped my bat involuntarily as the ball cracked me on the point of the left elbow. It had come back off the wicket like an off-break, and even Jackson had the grace to say he didn't think even he could move that much.

"I was rather ashamed of dropping my bat, and when the fielders asked me if I was OK I made the rash statement 'I'll be all right after the next ball.' I was, indeed, because the middle stump was flying out of the ground, and I was able to lick my wounds in the comfort of the dressing-room.

"'Jacko' has been called a slinger and was unlucky enough to come to his best at the same time as Trueman, Statham and Tyson. He might have played for England for ten years had he got the chance as a younger man. . . .

"Every year the county batsmen said hopefully 'Jackson won't be so fast this year' – 'not so good this year' – or even more hopefully' 'won't be playing this year'. But each year there he was with the new ball in his hand, and the devil take you if you didn't look sharp and at your best.

"Jack Robertson was the most refined batsman I have ever played against. Batting was reduced to its most economical limits in terms of movement, to a refinement known only to great artists. He never hit the ball hard, and yet beat the field easily to get his fours. . . .

"If he were to the pitch of the ball he would propel it effortlessly through the gaps between the fielders. If he were not to the pitch of the ball he would be content to push it slowly for one and proceed unhurriedly to the other end. His hook shot was similarly calm and graceful. Most players like to hook hard, to swat the ball away from in front of their eyes, but Jack Robertson would sway inside and just help the ball on its way.

"He was making many runs at the same time as the 'terrible twins', Compton and Edrich, and must have felt the coldness of their shadow, but whether they scored more or less than he did, they never made them more elegantly."

1
What is Style?

What is style? Of the eight differing versions in my dictionary I think Number Five is the one I am seeking: "Noticeable superior quality or manner especially in regard to breeding or fashion, distinction." Yes, that will serve, possibly with a dash of definition Number Two thrown in: "Collective characteristics of the (writing or diction or) artistic expression or way of presenting things or decorative methods proper to a person or school or period or subject."

Throughout its lengthening history cricket, whether you regard it as a sport, a way of life or an art form*, has been graced by a number of individuals whose "noticeable superior quality" in one or more of the basic skills has placed them apart from and above their more humdrum contemporaries. In the late 'seventies it has become the habit of the Press and television commentators to lament that English cricket is suffering from a dearth of such figures. *Plus ça change, plus c'est la même chose.* The representatives of the media, servants as they are to the cult of personality, have always regretted that they have not had a W. G. to eulogise, or a Bradman, or a Larwood, or a whoever. It seems to me that after a somewhat lean period of a remarkable few years, English cricket has recently been very adequately endowed with personalities. One cannot cavil at a team containing such charismatic and contrasting personalities as Tony Greig, Geoffrey Boycott, Alan Knott, Derek Randall, Derek Underwood and Bob Willis, all of whom possess style in greater or lesser degree.

But who are, and who have been, the true stylists of cricket? Who are the men who, over the years, have so imposed their ability and their personalities on the game that they are remembered not so much for their statistical achievements but for the *style* of their play, their influence on their contemporaries and those that came after them? Often, of

---

*I am presuming that anyone who regards cricket as a bore, a waste of time, or a pursuit for flannelled fools will not have bothered to have picked this book up in the first place.

course, the two have coincided in one personality; and the scorebook and *Wisden* have faithfully recorded for posterity that Dr W. G. Grace played 1493 first-class innings, 54,896 runs at an average of 39.55 and that Alec Bedser took 236 Test wickets for England, and 1924 wickets in first-class cricket; while at the same time acknowledging both cricket's and England's indebtedness to each for being a giant in his own way in his own day and age. The scorebook doesn't lie, but fine figures do not necessarily make stylish cricketers.

Is Geoffrey Boycott, for all the runs he has scored, a stylist? Or is he just, as someone once unkindly described him, a good defensive batsman who once played in spectacles but switched to contact lenses? Would you have made more of, say, Grace, than you would of, say, Bradman, of whom one critic said he was so good he drove you to the bar? Where does either of the Richards (black or white) stand in relation to Charlie Macartney or to Victor Trumper? Why was Spofforth "The Demon"? What made O'Reilly "The Tiger"? Does Underwood bear comparison with Verity, or Bedi with Rhodes? This is the type of question which has been asked as long as cricket has been played and writers have been writing about it. And is there a discernible link between Grace and Graveney; or between Kortright and Griffith and Thomson. . . ?

In seeking the answer to these, and more questions, I make no apology for delving into other people's writings. As one of the most prolific authors on cricket of this century, A. A. Thomson, wrote after penning his book on W. G., *The Great Cricketer,* "To crib from one book is plagiarism, to crib from a dozen is research." Over the past few months I have been variously captivated by the prose and poetry of Neville Cardus, fascinated by the breadth of vision of C. B. Fry, whose *Life Worth Living* is a masterpiece more enduring even than the memory of any of his magnificent innings, and sidetracked into a thousand byways by a hundred and one authors in the name of research. The more I have read the more fun I have had, but the less simple has analysis become, the more difficult my self-imposed task of finding guidelines through the forest of cricket's literature and history. So instead of the imposing genealogy of cricket style which I had intended to produce, I find myself plotting first of all the landmarks in the various stages of the sport's progress, and endeavouring thereafter to link them stepping-stone by stepping-stone, until perhaps some form of coherent pattern may emerge. And if you and I, gentle reader, digress along the way, it will be because cricket itself is the most digressive and discursive of pastimes.

But first, to return to my definition of style. Here is an example, from an essay by A. A. Thomson, of true "style" – style in the writing, style in the man, and in his batsmanship. I doubt if we'll better it anywhere in this book. The subject is E. R. Dexter, for playing for Sussex in 1960. He'd just made 96 and won the match for Sussex against Yorkshire; next, 111 at Worthing against Gloucestershire, "and again I watched the majestic strokes; easy, almost languid, infinitely graceful and except for the most enchanting late cuts, almost all in front of the wicket. In the Bank Holiday game against the old enemy, Middlesex, Dexter did it a third time, in an innings that for sheer aristocratic quality surpassed anything I had seen for years. With Don Smith, whose robust 80 was entitled to the highest praise, Dexter took the score from 42 for 4 into the three-hundreds and after tea the Middlesex fieldsmen, trying to stop drives which bit like serpents, may well have remembered where Dexter was born, and thought hard thoughts of the Viper of Milan. MacLaren, said Neville Cardus, did not hit the ball, he dismissed it from his presence. Woolley, said J. M. Barrie, whispered his wishes to the ball and it understood. And in 1960, whenever I see Dexter batting, I feel that, for a time at least, there is no impertinence in recalling great names and great phrases. Whatever I may think, I do not often shout there is nobody today like the old 'uns. Even if it is true it is irrelevant and, in any event, it seems churlish to keep rubbing it in. With Dexter at the wicket, I am certain that cricket is the same game I used to see in the brave days of old.

"In G. M. Trevelyan's *History of England* there is a much-quoted passage which lauds the English eighteenth-century way of life when 'squire, farmer, blacksmith and labourer, with the women and children, come to see the fun, were at ease together and happy all the summer afternoon. . . .' He also laments that in France peer and peasant never came together in that way. Yet if a French Duke of the *ancien régime* had learnt to bat – and what a pity none of them ever did – I toy with the fancy that he would have batted just as Dexter bats today; with *élan* and *panache,* with delicacy and supreme power, extravagantly, elegantly, a little disdainfully and above all, *ducally.* That touch of disdain sometimes gets him out to a haphazard stroke. Against Northamptonshire I saw him clean bowled at 17 after an innings which enshrined, like jewels in a small case, two of the noblest cover-drives seen by mortal eye since Hutton's or even Hammond's best. What makes it possible to mention his name in the same sentence as those of the immortals is his appearance of having all the time in the world to make his stroke – any stroke. Hobbs had three strokes for every ball and Trumper, his countrymen tell us, had five. Dexter undoubtedly has a minimum of two. . . ."

More than that, one of "Lord Ted's" boundaries smacked into Mr Thomson's elderly leg, raising a painful and multi-coloured bruise, whose "size and opulent vividness" were tributes to the sheer power of the stroke, for it appeared to be nonchalantly made.

But, to our landmarks or, possible more accurately, to the veritable lighthouses of cricket. From the 1870s to the First World War is generally known as the Golden Age of Cricket and was dominated for all but a dozen years of that time by the massive figure and extraordinary personality of Dr William Gilbert Grace; the years between the wars, when cricket prospered again and a small, dapper Australian reigned supreme – Donald Bradman; and after the Second World War, when Bradman had retired from active cricket to become a scratch golfer and a Stock Exchange wizard, there came what might well be known as the W. Era – W for West Indies, Weekes, Walcott and above all Worrell. Sir Frank Worrell, who forged the collection of brilliant individuals into a world-beating cricket team and in doing so gave a new nation a pride in and consciousness of its own abilities.

2
The Golden Age

One cannot but sympathise with the late C. B. Fry when, in 1902, he edited the quite magnificent *Book of Cricket*, a 254-page volume of cricketers of the day, copiously illustrated. Not only was he forced to write an assessment of his own abilities, a task which he accomplished with becoming modesty, for he was then at the very height of his considerable powers – in 1901 he staggered cricket by hitting centuries in six consecutive innings – but among his tasks had to write an assessment of W. G., then in his 54th year.

"So much has been written about Dr Grace", he began, "that nothing new remains to be said. Yet do people realise fully what a wonderful man this is? That any man at the age of fifty be worth a place in a county Eleven is remarkable enough; yet at this age Dr Grace is not only fit to play for the Gentlemen, but is considered worthy of a place in a representative England Eleven.

"There will never again be such a cricketer. A batsman may arise with as many strokes who may make as many runs. But who will ever keep his form like W. G.? As crafty a bowler may be found, but a recurrence of his like is impossible; it would demand a combination of qualities and powers too numerous and various.

"The main reason for his pre-eminence is his extraordinary physique, uniting as it does all the physical requirements of cricket. A huge frame, enormous strength, inexhaustible stamina, perfect accuracy of eye, extreme activity and quickness of limb – all these he had in his prime. But how wonderful that in one man should be united the height and reach of Gunn, the weight and muscles of Sandow, and the quickness almost of Ranjitsinhji? 'W. G.' seems to have enjoyed all the advantages of size and weight without any of the disadvantages. Even now one cannot help noticing his exceptional activity, in spite of his sixteen stone or so.

"He had the strength and reach, the quickness and agility to make every possible stroke; and also the eye, the perfectly accurate eye, that sees the ball directly it leaves the hand, and never gives the brain false information. His scores were wonderful, merely regarded as feats of endurance; the pace never killed him.

"But his physical qualities alone would not have made him the champion. Observation, intelligence, patience, perseverance, a level head, a thirst for knowledge – this and more went into his game.

"He used to be known as the best change bowler, and is not far from that still. He has a great command of length and a deceptive flight. He knows exactly how to attack each batsman, but for the most part he is content to bowl a good length on the leg side, trusting to his cleverly-arranged field for catches.

"In the mythology of cricket he is Jupiter the King."

So the old devil was an early proponent of, even if he didn't invent, the leg trap, as well as everything else he did.

W. G. – the great cricketer himself, at the finish of an off-drive.

16

What C. B. Fry did not mention in his eulogy was that some of W. G.'s massive scores were made when every shot had to be run full out, when, with the exception of balls that went full-pitch into the pavilion or clean out of the ground, there were no boundaries. The wickets, too, in the late nineteenth century, were nothing like the feather beds they are now, particularly at Lord's and The Oval. W. G. was once applauded to the echo when he blocked four diabolical shooters in a row at Lord's. He was also a fine fielder, who in his youth could throw three cricket balls in succession over 120 yards and then a fourth back over the same distance out of sheer exuberance. But he gave up fielding in the deep fairly young after an injury, and became a permanent fixture at point, except when he was bowling.

The picture that comes down over the years is of the most amazing vitality. A. A. Thomson quotes a country game in which a ball from him was skied hard and high to square leg. Yelling to the fieldsman nearly positioned there to get out of the way, W. G. came pounding forward like a charging buffalo. As with one hand stretched out in front of him he brought off an astounding catch at full gallop, the bewildered batsman was heard to mutter: "That chap won't be satisfied until he's keeping wicket to his own bowling."

In his first-class career W. G. took 877 catches, a total exceeded in the history of cricket by Kent's left-handed genius Frank Woolley alone.

Sir Neville Cardus wrote, in his *Cricket Discourse*, the introduction to a fine edition of cricket prints, co-edited by John Arlott, that W. G.'s great contribution to the technique of cricket was a synthesis of nearly all the principles of batsmanship established by his forerunners, accumulated by time and experiment, since the cricketers of Hambledon, Kent and Sussex changed "Bat and Ball" in the "Noblest" (and the most comprehensively skilful) of games, calling for a variety of skills, different methods of bowling, different methods of batsmanship.

"W. G.," he wrote, "to use a musical metaphor, took the themes invented by predecessors and elaborated them into a large-spanned symphony, a symphony not only of cricket, but one which could express English character, reflect the summer's light and shade, and relate itself to an environment."

'W. G. began his career as overarm bowling was legalised in the early 'sixties, having developed from underarm, lob bowling in the early part of the century through the round era of Alfred Mynn. H. S. Altham wrote of Mynn in 1926, "With a few deliberate and majestic strikes, bringing his arm round in a swing as smooth as a piston rod, he projected the ball assuredly faster than any English bowler of today." Admittedly, English fast bowling was at a low ebb after the 1914–18

17

war, but Harold Larwood had already burst on the scene, and he was no slow-coach.

Cardus's assessment was that, just as W. G. was the father of modern batsmanship, spreading his skills not only throughout the whole of England, but also to Australia, America, Canada and Ireland, so Alfred Shaw was the essential seminal influence on bowling. Shaw bowled in all nearly 25,000 four-ball overs, of which nearly 17,000 were maidens. He established the off-theory tactics which prevailed throughout the last quarter of the nineteenth century (in spite of W. G.'s success with leg-theory), the bulk of fieldsman concentrated on the off side of the wicket and the attack at or outside the off stump. A ball pitched on the leg side was a crude fall from grace, and more often than not the bowler had to apologise to his captain: Sorry, sir, it slipped."

Cardus records that when at Johannesburg, in 1906, England lost for the first time a Test match to South Africa, the match was a thriller. South Africa won by 1 wicket, and the winning hit was made from a ball pitched on the leg side of the wicket by Albert Relf.

P. F. (later Sir Pelham or more popularly "Plum") Warner, England's captain, cried from the bottom of his heart: "Oh, Albert, how could you?"

Cardus admits that the off-theory did to some extent shackle the batsman, but in common with every other student of the game he was emphatic that it was by no means as inhibiting as the nagging leg-theory bowling brought in the 1930s to try to contain the phenomenal powers of Bradman and persisting even today in one-day competitions. Off-theory did not cramp the really beautiful shots of cricket, the off-drive, square-cut, as in-swing bowling does. And it brought out the best in the fielding side too, with cover points like the lightning Trumper, points like Grace himself, and mid-offs and slip fielders easily equal to the Derek Randalls and Tony Greigs of today.

Indeed, in spite of the pitches and the vast number of wickets taken by the best of the bowlers, it was fairly commonplace for 3000 runs to be scored in a season by batsmen of the calibre of Grace, Fry and Ranjitsinhji even though games were often over the two days; just as 250 wickets a season was a not uncommon harvest of the bowlers of the quality of Shaw, Emmett and Freeman of Yorkshire, Hirst and Rhodes, Spofforth and Giffen and Jones of Australia, and so on. There was style in run-making and wicket-taking, but even then there was style too in the grim defence and the battle against odds. Perversely, the deeds of Scotton, who made 34 in 3¾ hours in the Test at The Oval in 1886 and once batted 1½ hours for nought, were almost as well celebrated, and suitable forerunners to the latter-day marathons of Trevor Bailey, Godfrey Evans, Bill Lawry of Australia and Jackie McGlew of South

Africa.

There was style, too, in the wicketkeeping, like that of Blackham of Australia, who "stood up to" (stood close behind the wicket) the fireballs of Frederick Robert Spofforth, the man who routed England in the famous "Ashes" Test of 1882; just as in the 'fifties Godfrey Evans was wont to stump batsmen "down the leg side" off the bowling of Alec Bedser. There was even style in the humour of Tom Lockyer, who kept wicket for Surrey, when he hinted to an earnest, trusting young batsman that he'd do well to pat down some unevenness in the pitch. When the batsman moved out of his crease to do so, Lockyer swept off the bails and appealed. Successfully.

W. G., not unnaturally, matched this. In the critical Test match of 1882, he nipped in and ran out S. P. Jones with a ball that the wicket-keeper had darted after and returned. Jones claimed the ball was "dead" and he'd only been "gardening" the pitch. But Robert Thoms, the best-known and fairest umpire of the day, gave him out. Jones was out-raged, but had to walk. In 1973, at a crucial moment of the first Test between England and West Indies at Kensington Oval, Port of Spain, Trinidad, Tony Greig duplicated this keen gamesmanship when he ran out Alvin Kallicharran off the last ball of the day, when the little left-hander had taken off his batting gloves and was heading peaceably for the pavilion. This almost caused an international incident, and Sang Hue, the umpire who gave Kallicharran out, was persuaded overnight to accept the dubious but politic argument that Greig had only meant his dramatic run-out and sky-splitting appeal as a joke. Kallicharran was reinstated the next morning, and moved, somewhat shakily, to a deserved century, being out shortly afterwards. This was the tiny man who once hooked Dennis Lillee, at his fastest and most furious, for 34 runs off 10 balls at The Oval.

Richie Benaud, former all-rounder, captain of Australia and now broadcaster supreme on cricket, once set out his "World XI". To his surprise, he discovered that all the batsmen in it had one thing in common: they were all great players off the *back* foot. Perhaps that sounds obvious, and it might have been more surprising had they *not*. But the foundation of all the true stylist batsmen has been an ability to score runs when, technically at least, they have been forced back on the defensive. "The trouble with that beggar," said a contemporary of W. G., "is that he can block 'em all right – all the way to the boundary."

W. G. himself, from the age of seven, was nurtured in the merits of a straight bat and a strong defence by his father, old Dr Grace, and his Uncle Pocock, his mother's brother Alfred, who would walk twelve miles a day to coach his nephews, W. G. and E. M., on the wicket laid out in the garden at Downend in West Gloucestershire. He and his brothers would bowl to each other, and the fielders would be his sisters and a couple of cricketing dogs. Their severest critic was their mother. One of the most cherished documents in cricket history is the letter in which she recommended E. M. to George Parr, the captain of the nomadic All-England Eleven and told him, prophetically, that she had another boy growing up who would do better than his brother because his defence was sounder.

The pictures of W. G., mostly taken when he was well past his best, show him extremely well anchored by his strong right leg. This is not to say he would not leave his crease and leap down the pitch with elephantine ease to thump the ball back over the slow bowler's head; but from the firm base of the right leg he could cut, cover-drive or force away to any part of the leg field any ball even fractionally short of a length. As Benaud says, all the really great batsmen have had this ability. Think of Clive Lloyd, the recent West Indian captain, whose untutored brilliance enables him to hit the ball unbelievably hard and unbelievably late – almost posthumously, as they used to say. Think of the elegance of Garfield Sobers, the merciless striking of Bradman, the fluency of Neil Harvey and you'll see what I mean. The most imperious shot I ever saw in my life, apart possibly from any Hutton off-drive, was a straight drive by Walter Hammond for six into the pavilion at Lord's – off the back foot.

Kumar Shri Ranjitsinhji, after W. G. the major exponent of style in the Golden Age of cricket, first came to prominence as a member of the Cambridge XI in 1892. He brought to the strictly English game realms of Oriental wizardry and loveliness and hidden power. This is Fry's contemporary assessment of his abilities: "His great fame as a batsman is not only due to his success as measured in runs, but also, and in chief, to the originality and peculiar charm of his style. Nothing is as effective as a striking result produced without any apparent effort.

"There are many batsmen who make some one stroke with such wonderful ease and effect that all their other strokes receive in comparison but scant appreciation. In Ranjitsinhji's case every turn of his bat has this appearance of extreme facility, to such a degree, indeed, that his style seems almost casual or careless. The distinctive trait of his cricket is an electric quickness both in the conception and execution of his strokes. Thereby he is able to do such things as a slower wrist and eye dare not attempt. In making the ordinary strokes, he differs from the run of batsmen in that he judges the flight of the ball about half as soon again, and can therefore shape for his strokes more readily and with more certainly. At the same time he need not, owing to his marvellous rapidity of movement, allow himself as much margin

20

for error as others find necessary. And it is this quickness that enables him to take, even on the fastest of wickets, the most unheard-of liberties without fatal results.

"Who, for instance, but Ranji can hit across a fast straight ball without either being bowled or making an appalling mishit? Yet Ranji finds not the slightest difficulty in doing so. This is perhaps his most noticeable stroke. He has a miraculous knack of timing the ball accurately from the pitch, flicks it round to the on side with supple yet terrific power. He meets the slightly overpitched delivery with a similar hit reaching right out so as to clip the ball before it pitches.

"There never has been a greater master of cutting and of legplay. In cutting, his faculty for quick and accurate timing gives him the power of varying and placing his stroke, as well as of making it with force and precision. His leg strokes are sometimes called 'glances', but they are really wrist-strokes, as the ball boes not merely hit the bat, but is turned aside with a lithe forcing movement.

"His forward play is somewhat unorthodox, as he walks out to the ball as he hits, but is nevertheless strong and safe. He can drive finely

Ranjitsinhji's leg-glance – "really a wrist-stroke", but a touch of ballet about the feet.

in all directions when in the mood; indeed, at his best, he can use every stroke in the game.

"He is a beautiful fielder in any position. He excels at point or in the slips, where there is scope for his quickness; but, as he can pick up a ball very clean, catch anything and throw well, he is almost equally good as extra-cover or in the long field."

That description, one must note in the cause of establishing lineages, could well describe the magic of Denis Compton of later date, or even, in the past year or two, the batting of Alan Knott at its very best, as demonstrated in the Nottingham Test of 1977, when he played his greatest innings for England and mesmerised the Australian bowlers. He even contrived to get himself out off an upper-cut inches short of a six.

Ranjitsinhji played for Sussex from 1895 to 1908, heading the averages every year bar two (in the days when Fry was supreme) and scoring more than 17,000 runs for the county at an average exceeding 65. In all matches he scored 23,415, average 57.67. In 1899 and 1900 he made over 3000 runs in the English first-class season and in one match, for Sussex against Yorkshire at Brighton, he obtained two separate hundreds – 100 and 125 not out – *on the same day*!

When Ranji, as an Indian prince, first arrived in England, he found an immense difference between the cricket he had been playing in India to the current first-class game. He'd never seen overarm bowling, for one, and cheerfully admitted that "to see men calmly standing up to fast bowling and not running away from it astonished me very much. When I was at practice at Cambridge, Sharpe, the Surrey bowler, used to say to me 'Look here, you know, sir, if you can't keep those legs of yours still I shall have to peg them down.'" He cured himself by paying Tom Hayward, the Surrey professional, to bowl to him.

Ranjitsinhji was the first of a long line of cricketers from the Indian sub-continent who have entertained and dazzled the crowds over the years. His nephew, Duleepsinhji, arrived on the scene in the 'thirties to emulate his illustrious forbear, and subsequently there have been the Pataudis, a whole string of Mohammads from Hanif onwards, and Alis and Khans, the latest of whom – Majid – graced Glamorgan and Pakistan in the 'sixties and 'seventies with his arrogant ease.

Any selection of batsmen from the Golden Age must leave out a score of players who these days would be welcome in any cricket team in the world, with the possible exception of West Indies.

There was Gilbert Jessop, who, as his discoverer, W. G., prophesied, became the greatest hitter the world has ever seen – though, strangely, he does not hold the record for the fastest century (that was P. G. Fender in 35 minutes) – and who in one inter-varsity match hit 42 off 14 balls; his style, according to Fry, was unique. Unlike most hitters, he held his bat at the stance with his hands somewhat apart on the handle, clasping and unclasping his fingers in nervous energy. He crouched over his bat "like a panther about to spring". If the ball was well up he would hit firmfooted, but he preferred the shorter ball, to which he would "unslip" and dance down the pitch to hit "on the up" in any direction. He square-cut with withering power, and to sweep to leg he would lie down and sweep round with a horizontal bat. A foretaste of whom? Rohan Kanhai?

Then there was Lionel Palairet, all elegance and ease from Somerset, "the most beautiful batsman of the day, that is to say his style of play combines to a greater degree than any other batsman pure grace and elegance with full effectiveness and power." His was, it was said, the champagne of cricket. And R. H. Spooner, the cricketing forbear of Dexter, in arrogant superiority his equal if not quite so devastating in his power.

Power and purpose. Jessop's on-drive eschewed elegance but went for four.

What, too, of Arthur Shrewsbury, the greatest professional batsman of his day, and (if such a contrast can be made at 80 years distance) to cricket then what Geoffrey Boycott is today? Listen to this contemporary description: "It has been said of him that he has reduced the game to an absolute science – almost a certainty; and that the secret of his success is his perfect judgment of the length and pace of every ball that is bowled to him. He has been accused of spoiling cricket and of ruining the game in Nottingham. No shrewd judge of the game would question Shrewsbury's cricket . . . his pre-eminent trait is his mastery of the back-stroke. He has strong, quick wrists and uses them well. He can hook very finely, and is a master of placing his strokes. . . . Arthur Shrewsbury has played some of the greatest innings in the history of the game. . . ." Substitute Boycott for Shrewsbury and add that no-one in Yorkshire would ever dare to opine that "our Geoffrey" had ruined cricket and you don't have a bad description, do you?

And what, too, of Archie (A. C.) MacLaren, captain of Lancashire and England, hitter of 424 in one innings, who was for the first decade of the century what Walter Hammond was to the third; or J. T. Tyldesley, or Pelham Warner, or Robert Abel, the "Guv'nor" of Surrey, who made his 2000 runs season in, season out. Or. . . ?

The names trip off the mind and onto the typewriter, for the Golden Age was an age not only of batsmen but of bowlers too.

In the early 1900s they said that Alfred Shaw, with whom we have already made acquaintance, was in his prime the most accurate bowler in the world. He was medium-pace right-arm, but never a genuine swing bowler – the Golden Age hardly produced them, as in those days a cricket ball was new only at the start of the match, and was then never changed until it split in two no matter how many hundreds Dr Grace or A. G. Steel hit off it. In the autumn of his days Shaw was a superb coach and still, with ball, an artist and a genius. And as such he merited C. B. Fry's compliment: "He is the best man in the world to meet if you happen to have been bowled first ball."

The really fast bowlers of English cricket of the time included S. M. J. Woods, an Australian who settled in England after being educated at Cambridge and came to captain Somerset, Tom Richardson and Bill Lockwood of Surrey, and a lovely character named Arthur Mold, of Lancashire, who bowled fast off a four-pace run and could "bowl the unplayable ball even off a perfect wicket".

It is perhaps worth noticing that of these four, only Woods was an amateur. Most of the great batsmen of the period were amateurs in name if not in genuine fact; although the fastest bowler of them all, C. J. Kortright of Essex, was genuinely proud of the fact that he never did a day's work in his life. Perhaps in general the amateurs left the

24

Sammy Woods – beer, lobsters and ten wickets.

really hard work to the pros.

Samuel Moses James Woods was a great all-round athlete. He was called on by the Australians in 1888 and played three Tests against England; subsequently he played for England against South Africa and represented England at rugby football. He got his county cap at soccer and bowls, as well, and sustained a serious injury at mixed hockey. Alan Gibson, quite my favourite cricket-writer after R. C. Robertson-Glasgow, in a delightful article in Denzil Batchelor's *Great Cricketers*, records that one of Woods' most famous remarks was that draws were only of any use for swimming in.

In those days by far the most important match of the season was the annual match, Gentlemen v Players. It had more prestige than an international, and many a fine cricketer was selected for England before he was given the honour of appearing at Lord's in the annual showpiece.

In this particular year Woods was captain of the Gentlemen. He set the Players 500 to win and when time was up they had tied the scores, with 2 wickets left, Tom Hayward and J. T. Brown of Yorkshire getting most of the runs. The umpires were about to take off the bails when Woods himself took the ball for an extra over. The Players won, and Woods was criticised, but, says Gibson, criticism had about as much effect on him as a peashooter on the Great Pyramid.

On another occasion at Cambridge, Woods shared rooms with Gregor MacGregor, also a Cambridge captain and later an England wicket-keeper. The University were playing an eleven of international standard, raised by C. I. Thornton, a noted hard-hitting cricketer, and they invited him and about half a dozen of his team to breakfast. The bill of fare was headed by draught beer and hot lobsters. The visitors were horrified, so they were duly provided with coffee and bacon and eggs, while Woods and MacGregor ate the lobsters and drank the beer between them. After that they started cricket and Woods took all 10 wickets in an innings.

(It was a feat of which in a later year Freddie Trueman would have been proud, although the ability to sink vast quantities of alcohol seems to be natural to fast bowlers. On the 1956–57 MCC tour of South Africa I once sat up until three o'clock in the morning with Brian Statham drinking beer in Bulawayo; and in the morning held my head and mourned for my lost stomach while Statham took 5 Rhodesian wickets before lunch in a sustained spell of hostile fast bowling.)

Tom Richardson was the idol of Surrey, a sturdy six-footer with the moustache of a Lothario and long, springing run. He was able to keep up his full pace for over after over, day after day, delivering the ball

A picture of honest toil – Tom Richardson into his last stride.

with a swinging rotary action. His pace seemed to come from his back and hips, and of today's bowlers one would liken him to Mike Hendrick of Derbyshire, or possibly the Australian Max Walker (in appearance, not action, for Walker's off-the-wrong-foot action, like Mike Procter's, is unusual).

Sir Neville Cardus, in his *A Cricketer's Book,* paints an unforgettable portrait of Richardson: "On 26 June 1902, Old Trafford was a place of Ethiopic heat and the crowd that sat there in an airless world saw J. T. Tyldesley flog the Surrey bowlers all over the field. Richardson attacked from the Stratford end, and at every over's finish he wiped the sweat from his brow and felt his heart beating hammer-strokes. Richardson had all his fielders on the off side, save one, who 'looked out' at mid-on. And once (and once only) he bowled a long-hop to Tyldesley, who swung on his heels and hooked it high and far into the long field. The Surrey fieldsman at mid-wicket saw something pass

27

him and with his eyes helplessly followed the direction of the hit. 'One boundary more or less won't count on a day like this', it was possible to imagine the sweltering fellow telling himself. 'Besides, Johnny's plainly going to get 'em anyhow.'

"The ball slackened pace on the boundary's edge. Would it just roll home? The crowd tried to cheer it to the edge of the field. Then one was aware of heavy thuds on the earth. Some Surrey man after all had been fool enough to think that a desperate spurt and boundary saved might be worthwhile, blistering sun despite. Who on earth was the stout but misguided sportsman?

"Heaven be praised, it was Richardson himself. He had bowled the ball; he had been bowling balls, and his fastest, for nearly two hours. His labours in the sun had made ill those who sat watching him. And here he was, pounding along the outfield, after a hit from his own bowling.

"The writer sat on the 'Popular' side of the ground, under the scoreboard, as the ball got home a foot in advance of Richardson. The impetus of his run swept him over the edge of the grass, and to stop himself he put out his arms and grasped the iron rail. He laughed – the handsomest laugh in the world – and said 'Thank you' to somebody who threw the ball back to him. His face was wet, his breath scant. He was the picture of honest toil. With the ball in his hands again he trotted back to the wicket and once more went through the travail of bowling at J. T. Tyldesley on a pitiless summer's day."

On this day his Surrey partner, Bill Lockwood, was a more awkward customer to face, rather as Bob Willis may be compared with Mike Hendrick in the current England team. He appeared very fast off the pitch, and was able to make the ball wobble in the air deceptively. He was said to be able to bowl batsmen out even before the ball had pitched. "His action in running up and delivering the ball is a picture of ease and grace and power. He runs with a long springy stride, bounding from the ground like an india-rubber ball. His delivery is beautifully free and strong. He bowls over the wicket but runs so wide that he is often no-balled for encroaching on the return crease." He was also a useful batsman.

Arthur Mold, the Alec Bedser of his time, was one of the pillars of Lancashire's success in the formative years of the County Championship. From 1889 to 1896 he took more than a hundred wickets a season – 207 in 1894 and 214 the following year. His secret, like Bedser's, was in the smoothness of his delivery and his great accuracy. But whereas Bedser's attack was often concentrated on the in-swinger, Mold was a devotee of off-theory, bowling outside the off stump to a packed off field. Often there would be only one, or at the most two, fieldsmen on the leg side.

Three or four yards faster than all of these was Charles Kortright, the thunderer from Essex who is celebrated for once conceding six leg-byes off an unfortunate batsman's left ear. The ball flew off his head, over wicketkeeper's and longstop's head and past the sightscreen. It was probably at Wallingford, which has always been a small ground, but still. . . . Through all the decades, there has been at least one man whose name has spelt terror to batsmen and filled grounds all over the world – Ernest Jones, Gregory, McDonald, McCormick, Lindwall, Lillee and Thomson of Australia; Larwood, Trueman, Tyson, Statham of England; Heine, Adcock and Pollock of South Africa; Constantine, Hall, Griffith, Roberts, Holding, Daniel and now Croft of West Indies. Kortright was the name of the fast game in the early years of this century. His rivalry with the ageing W. G. was famous.

Playing for Essex against Gloucestershire, he beat W. G. all ends up

The only known action picture of C. J. Kortright – at Edgbaston in 1895. Some of his fire must have gone – see where the wicketkeeper is standing.

Hirst (left) and Rhodes (right). All-rounders, left-handers, and near

in one innings, having several appeals for l.b.w. and caught-behind turned down. Eventually, with a yorker the speed of light, he smashed the middle and off stumps out of the ground. As the dismissed W. G. passed him, taking off his gloves on the way to the pavilion, Kortright murmured, in mock incredulity: "You're not going, Doctor? There's one stump still standing." W. G. said he'd never been so insulted in all his life, and didn't forgive him until Kortright, who was no batsman, partnered the Old Man in a desperate but eventually unsuccessful last-wicket attempt to stave off defeat of the Gentlemen by the Players. Or perhaps it was when, in his "Jubilee" year, in the late summer of his life, he hit an attack including Kortright for a century.

But Kortright, for all his competitiveness, revered W. G. Cardus (again) tells of a young university batsman who came to the wicket, took guard, and then took his stance, like W. G., with his front toe cocked in the air. (It was the one affectation W. G. possessed at the wicket, a product of his enormous enthusiasm to "get at it".)

geniuses?

"I was about to bowl," said Kortright, "so I said to him: 'Put your toe down; I allow nobody except W. G. to face me with his toe up.' But the young cove declined to put his toe down, which was an impertinence to me. I sent him a yorker bang on that cocked-up toe, and he had to be carried back to the pavilion."

The feats on an extraordinary pair of all-rounders, George Hirst and Wilfred Rhodes, Yorkshire and England, still live in the page of *Wisden*. Hirst, whose first-class career extended from 1889 to 1929 – yes, 40 years – still stands alone as the only man who ever took 200 wickets and made 2000 runs in a season, the "double double". In all he took 2739 wickets and scored 36,323 runs, and did the simple "double" (1000 runs, 100 wickets) no fewer than fourteen times. His partner Rhodes did that double sixteen times, and in *his* career, which lasted eight years less, spanning the period 1898 to 1930, still holds the record for the number of wickets taken – 4187 at an average of 16.71.

I mention these figures, courtesy of *Wisden,* not because of any love of statistics (which, like Samuel Woods, I'm always getting wrong anyway) but to point out that the last cricketer to perform the "double" in a season was Fred Titmus, of Middlesex, in 1967, twelve years ago. And it is 28 years since Bob Appleyard was the last man to take 200 wickets in a season; such is the age of specialisation. (Tony Greig, reckoned a good enough all-rounder to captain England in 1976, scored 765 runs and took 36 wickets in that year).

Rhodes, incidentally, shared in an opening partnership for England (with Jack Hobbs) of 323, which was not broken for 36 years; and another with the meteoric R. E. Foster, of 130 for the last wicket, at Sydney in 1903, – which is still a Test record. Yes, he batted at both Number 1 and Number 11 for his country. Another record.

It was in the fifth Test in the summer of 1902 at The Oval (Jessop's Test, in which Jessop hit 104 out of 139 in an hour and a quarter) when Rhodes, Number 11 as he played then, went out to joint Hirst with 15 runs remaining. They did, in fact, make the runs, but not all in singles, as has often been reported.

Hirst, bold and imperturbable, began his career as a quick left-arm bowler, slowing to what we now know as orthodox left-arm. His free, swinging action delivered a natural leg-cutter which on crumbling pitches broke sharply away from the bat, and could be devastating. He was a fine mid-off, too, who would catch anything and check even the nimblest of batsmen with his speed and anticipation over the ground. His imitators used to practise with a box on the pitch to try to acquire the sort of swerve he could impart to the ball.

Rhodes, on the other hand, was arguably the best genuine slow left-arm spin bowler cricket has ever seen. He could disguise his pace and spin the ball viciously with his fingers. Alf Gover, who still passes on his years of collected wisdom to youngsters at his cricket school in Wandsworth, tells of the searing experience he once had when he was sent out to save Surrey from annihilation by Yorkshire. The score was 94 for 9, and Jack Hobbs had 71 of them. Hobb's resourceful farming of the bowling had for once failed and Gover was left to face a whole over from Wilfred Rhodes. "There has never been an over in history which came so near to dismissing a batsman six times without actually doing so," reports A. A. Thomson of the incident. "Every delivery was as guileful as a serpent and how each one failed to dislodge the bails nobody, least of all Mr Gover, will ever know. At the end of this lurid over, with the batsman still staring in dazed incredulity at his undisturbed stumps, Hobbs strolled across to him. 'Stay at that end, Alf,' he said. 'You've got Wilfred taped. Best bowler in England he can't even find your bat.'"

Rhodes – Verity – Lock – Underwood. The line of succession is easy

32

to see. Not so easy is to find a successor to Sydney Barnes. Of the right-handers, after Mold and before Tate, came Sydney Barnes, generally assessed as the finest fast-medium bowler of his, or any other, day. His run-up was short, his action high and springy, his followthrough beautifully balanced. Like Tate, but even more so, he made the ball appear to gain pace off the pitch rather than slow down, in defiance of all science. Most of all though he was an innovator, like W. G. and B. J. T. Bosanquet, of whom more in a moment. When he began bowling fast-medium, Barnes knew that the most dangerous ball of all was the one that moved away from the bat. Slow leg-break bowlers could do it and left-armers, but your average right-hander of the day fast, medium and slow, relied on the breakback, which they used to call, incorrectly, "Body spin".

Barnes came to the conclusion, according to Ian Peebles, who had it from the old man's lips, that the only way a pace bowler could make the ball run away to the slips was to bowl the leg-break in the same manner as the off-break; without the rotation of the bent wrist. He set about finding out how to do it and became one of the very rare cricketers really to have succeeded. He managed to deliver the leg-break at fast-medium pace with the wrist straight and the palm of the hand towards the batsman. He spent some years experimenting, and then, he said, it came to him quite suddenly. Once accomplished, it was as though he had penetrated the sound barrier, and he had no further difficulty, the only questions resolving themselves into refinement and application.

Peebles says the technique must not be confused with that of the modern "cutter", which is to flip the fingers over the surface of the ball and impart enough spin to give the ball a little bias in advantageous conditions. Barnes gripped the ball firmly between first and third fingers and *spun* it. His advantage over the latter-day swervers, or swingers of the ball was that the latter have always been dependent on outside factors, such as the condition of the ball, the humidity of the atmosphere, the greenness of the pitch. Barnes's spin was equally potent with the old or new ball in any weather, and he added, of course, the elements of pace, life and accuracy. It must have been like meeting a deadly accurate Doug Wright, only faster and more deceptive.

Peebles once asked that genius of the 'twenties, Charlie Macartney, just how good was Barnes. "I'll tell you how good he was," he replied. "In 1912 I went out to bat and told the chaps I was going out to hit this chap Barnes for six." He paused to give weight to the point. "I had to wait until I was 68 before I did."

Barnes, with Frank R. Foster, formed one of the most formidable Test bowling combinations ever known. They swept the Australians aside by four matches to one in 1910–11, and Barnes took 34 wickets to

Out on his own. Sydney Barnes, the greatest bowler yet.

Foster's 32. They made a fine contrast – Barnes tall and gaunt, with a dour demeanour, hiding the menace of his spin and swerve concealed in his large right hand; Foster, left-arm, also tall, confident and aggressive. Foster made more impact on Australian cricket in the years just before the war than anyone else, causing several bowlers to try to alter their own styles to copy his, and few with any effective results.

Foster had a very short run-up, round the wicket, with a delivery which was very quick – almost genuinely fast. He bowled from the very extent of the crease, bringing the ball abruptly across the pitch from off to leg, aiming mostly at the leg stump, somehimes straightening up, sometimes going straight on – an extremely hostile bowler, difficult to play and even more difficult to score runs off.

The description calls to mind, in particular, Gary Gilmour at his very best in England in 1975, Sobers and Julien of West Indies, and England's John Lever, although his is the typical swing bowler's run-up, to the critical spectator's view at least ten yards too long for his pace. Foster's leg-theory brought up to date the methods used by W. G. Grace. (Twenty years later, the changes in the l.b.w. law designed to curb the massive scoring of Bradman, Hammond and the like were a significant step in ending off-theory, which had prevailed for some 50 years. In some ways, Foster was the forerunner of bodyline, introduced by Jardine and carried out with deadly accuracy by Larwood, that brought Australia closer to physical conflict with Britain than at any time until the advent of Mr Kerry Packer.)

Like Barnes, B. J. T. Bosanquet of the unpronounceable name (say Bose'n'ket) began his cricketing life as a fast right-arm bowler. He was, said Fry, the exception to the general rule that decreed that University bowling was always weak, sometimes weaker than others. Mr Bosanquet, said Fry, would have been an addition to the bowling strength of any side. He bowled with a high, easy swing, round the wicket, the ball "going away" with the arm as often as not, and he was particularly fond of the "bumper" on uneven wickets. He was a useful bat, who thumped the ball hard, and could "make runs fast and hit good-length balls".

Even so, when he went under P. F. Warner on the Australian tour of 1903 he was as much a dark horse as Tyson was to the Australians in the 1950s. Except, of course, that Tyson was sheer speed and Bosanquet had invented the googly.

In the fourth Test at Sydney he took 6 for 51 in Australia's second innings, winning the match for England. Three were stranded yards down the pitch and stumped, almost apologetically, by Lilley. Fifteen months later virtually the same team succumbed to Bosanquet to the tune of 8 for 107.

The Australians to this day still sometimes call the ball after him –

the "Bosie". The googly is, defined simply, an off-break bowled with a leg-break action, and at the moment is (almost) a forgotten art in first-class cricket, though it still does occasional duty in club cricket and on the village green.

As Bosanquet bowled it, it was new and revolutionary. He claimed that he had learned it from playing "twisti-twosti" with a tennis ball on a billiard table (Bosanquet played billiards brilliantly, an accomplish-

A precise action shot of B. J. T. Bosanquet. Note the stride, the immaculate sideways-on position, the balancing left arm and the relaxed, deceptive wrist.

36

ment which he handed on to his son, the television personality), the object being to deceive your opponent, sitting opposite, into guessing wrongly which way it would bounce.

Having practised assiduously with a cricket ball, he tried out his new "twist" in a county match for Middlesex in 1903 and recounted how his first victim committed suicide by stumping after watching the beastly thing bounce four times. He was himself puzzled by his own success and wrote: "Poor old googly. It has been subjected to ridicule, abuse, contempt, incredulity and survived them all. After all, what is the googly? It is merely a ball with an ordinary break produced by an extraordinary method."

But that wasn't the half of it. Anyone who has played against a good googly bowler (Ian Chappell, the former Australian captain, bowls them now for a lark and Kerry O'Keeffe does it quite seriously) knows how difficult it is to "read" his spin. You play where the ball, by all the normal rules, should be, and it isn't. You read it wrongly, and you're still playing it to the off when your leg bail hits the floor or short leg takes the catch.

Bosanquet was a true all-rounder. Among his other accomplishments he gained a half-Blue for throwing the hammer, scored two hundreds in one match of Middlesex, and in 1904, his googliest year, he did the double. His own verdict on the googly was, when asked if he did not think it was really illegal: "Oh no. Only immoral."

For the last word on the googly, I would like to include a superb piece of writing by one of its better exponents, Arthur Mailey. Apart from being one of Australia's greatest spinners, Mailey had an acute knowledge of cricket and cricketers, a subtle sense of humour, and could express himself as articulately in his own way as could C. B. Fry himself. This story illustrates all those qualities; besides, quite by the way, it gives almost an inch-by-inch description of what a googly does, and why, and how you bowl it. At the same time it will act as a suitable bridge for me to venture across into the wider world of cricket which experienced, and exploited, and enjoyed Mr Bosanquet's invention just as wholeheartedly as the English. Aside from which, I like the story. It comes from Mailey's autobiography *10 for 66 and All That:*

"Although at this time I had never seen Trumper play, on occasions I trudged from Waterloo across the Sandhills to the Sydney Cricket Ground and waited at the gate to watch the players coming out. Once I had climbed on a train and actually sat opposite my hero for three stops. I would have gone further but having no money I did not want to take the chance of being kicked in the pants by the conductor. Even so, I had been taken half a mile out of my way.

"In my wildest dreams I never thought I would ever speak to

Trumper let alone play against him. I am fairly phlegmatic by nature but between the period of my selection and the match I must have behaved like a half-wit.

"Right up to my first Test match I always washed and pressed my own flannels, but before this match I pressed them not once, but several times. On the Saturday I was up with the sparrows looking anxiously at the sky. It was a lovely morning but it still might rain. Come to that, lots of things could happen in ten hours – there was still a chance that Vic would be taken ill or knocked down by a tram or twist his ankle or break his arm. . . .

"My thoughts were interrupted by a vigorous thumping on the back gate. I looked out of the washhouse-bathroom-woodshed-workshop window and saw that it was the milkman who was kicking up the row.

"'Hey,' he roared. 'Yer didn't leave the can out. I can't wait around here all day. A man should pour it in the garbage tin – that'd make yer wake up a bit.'

"On that morning I couldn't have cared whether he poured the milk in the garbage tin or all over me. I didn't belong to this world. I was playing against the great Victor Trumper. Let the milk take care of itself.

"I kept looking at the clock. It might be slow – or it might have stopped. I'd better whip down to the Zetland Hotel and check up. Anyhow, I mightn't bowl at Trumper after all. He might get out before I come on. Or I mightn't get a bowl at all – after all I don't put myself on. Wonder what Trumper's doing this very minute . . . bet he's not ironing his flannels. He's probably got two sets of flannels anyway. Perhaps he's at breakfast, perhaps he's eating bacon and eggs. Wonder if he knows I'm playing against him? Don't suppose he's ever heard of me. Wouldn't worry him anyhow, I shouldn't think. Gosh, what a long morning. Think I'll dig the garden. No, I won't, I want to keep fresh. Think I'll lie down for a bit . . . better not, I might fall off to sleep and be late.

"The morning did not pass in this way. Time just stopped. I couldn't bring myself to do anything in particular and yet I couldn't settle to the thought of not doing anything. I was bowling to Trumper and I was not bowling to Trumper. I was early and I was late. In fact, I think I was slightly out of my mind.

"I didn't get to the ground so very early after all, mainly because it would have been impossible for me to wait around so near the scene of Trumper's appearance – and yet for it to rain or news to come that something had prevented Vic from playing.

"'Is he here?' I asked Harry Goddard, our captain, the moment I did arrive at the ground.

Arthur Mailey – he spun words as well as cricket-balls.

"'Is who here?' he countered.

"My answer was probably a scornful and disgusted look. I remember it occurred to me to say 'Julius Caesar, of course!' but that I stopped myself being cheeky because this was one occasion when I couldn't afford to be.

"Paddington won the toss and took the first knock.

"When Trumper went out to bat, Harry Goddard said to me: 'I'd better keep you away from Vic. If he starts on you he'll probably knock you out of grade cricket.'

"I was inclined to agree with him yet at the same time I didn't fear punishment from the master batsman. All I wanted to do was to bowl at him. I suppose in their time other ambitious youngsters have wanted to play on the same stage with Henry Irving, or sing with Caruso or Melba, to fight with Napoleon or sail the sea with Columbus. It wasn't conquest I desired. I simply wanted to meet my hero on common ground.

"Vic, beautifully clad in creamy, loose-fitting but well-tailored flannels, left the pavilion with his bat tucked under his left arm and in the act of donning his gloves. Although slightly pigeon-toed in the left foot he had a springy athletic walk and a tendency to shrug his shoulders every few minutes, a habit I understand he developed through trying to loosen the shirt off his shoulders when it became soaked with sweat during his innings.

"Arriving at the wicket, he bent his bat handle almost to right angle, walked up the pitch, prodded about six yards of it, returned to the batting crease and asked the umpire for 'two legs', took a quick glance in the direction of fine leg, shrugged his shoulders again and settled in to his stance.

"I was called on to bowl sooner than I expected. I suspect now that Harry Goddard changed his mind and decided to put me out of my misery early in the piece.

"Did I ever bowl that first ball? I don't remember. My hand was in a whirl. I really think I fainted and the secret of the mythical first ball has been kept over all these years to save me from embarrassment. If the ball *was* sent down it must have been hit for six, or at least four, because I was awakened from my trance by the thunderous booming 'Gabba who roared: 'O for a strong arm and a walking stick!'

"I do remember the next ball. It was, I imagined, a perfect leg-break. When it left my hand it was singing sweetly like a humming-top. The trajectory couldn't have been more graceful if designed by a professor of ballistics. The tremendous leg-spin caused the ball to swing and curve from the off and move in line with the middle and leg stump. Had I bowled this particular ball at any other batsman I would have turned my back early in its flight and listened for the death rattle. However, consistent with my idolisation of the champion, I watched his every movement.

"He stood poised like a panther ready to spring. Down came his left foot to within a foot of the ball. The bat, swung from well over his shoulders, met the ball just as if fizzed off the pitch, and the next sound I heard was a rapping on the off-side fence.

"It was the most beautiful shot I have ever seen.

"The immortal 'Gabba made some attempt to say something but his voice faded away into the soft gurgle one hears at the end of a kookaburra's song. The only person on the ground who did not watch the course of the ball was Victor Trumper. The moment he played it he turned back, smacked down a few tufts of grass and prodded his way back to the batting crease. He knew where the ball was going.

"What were my reactions?

"Well, I never expected that ball or any other ball I could ever produce to get Trumper's wicket. But that being the best ball a bowler of my type could spin into being, I thought that at least Vic might have been forced to play a defensive shot, particularly as I was a stranger too and it might have been to his advantage to use discretion rather than valour.

"After I had bowled one or two other reasonably good balls without success I found fresh hope in the thought that Trumper had found Bosanquet, creator of the 'wrong 'un' or 'bosie' (which I think a better name), rather puzzling. This left me with one shot in my locker, but if I didn't use it quickly I would be taken out of the firing line. I decided, therefore, to try this most undisciplined and cantankerous creation of the great B. J. T. Bosanquet – not, as many think, as a compliment to the inventor but as the gallant farewell, so to speak, of a warrior who refused to surrender until all his ammunition was spent.

"Again fortune was on my side in that I bowled the ball I had often dreamed of bowling. As with the leg-break, it had quite sufficient spin to curve in the air and break considerably after making contact with the pitch. If anything, it might have had a little more top-spin, which would cause it to drop rather suddenly. The sensitivity of a spinning ball against a breeze is governed by the amount of spin imparted, and if a ball bowled at a certain pace drops on a certain spot, one bowled with identical pace but with more top-spin should drop eighteen inches or two feet shorter.

"For this reason I thought the difference in the trajectory and ultimate landing of the ball might provide a measure of uncertainty in Trumper's mind. Whilst the ball was in flight this reasoning appeared to be indicated by Trumper's initial movement. As at the beginning of my over he sprang in to attack but did not realise that the ball, being an off-break, was floating away from him and dropping a little quicker. Instead of his left foot being closed to the ball it was a foot out of line.

"In a split second Vic grasped this and tried to make up the deficiency with a wider swing of the bat. It was then I could see a passage-way to the stumps with our 'keeper, Con Hayes, ready to claim his victim. Vic's bat came through like a flash but the ball passed between his bat and his legs, missed the leg stump by a fraction and the bails were whipped off with the great batsman at least two yards out of his ground.

"Vic had made no attempt to scramble back. He knew the ball had beaten him and was prepared to pay the penalty, and although he had little chance of regaining his crease on this occasion I think he would have acted similarly if his back foot had been only an inch from safety.

"As he walked past me he smiled, patted the back of his bat, and said: 'It was too good for me.'

"There was no triumph in me as I watched the receding figure. I felt like a boy who had killed a dove."

Although Australia has produced some of the very greatest batsman of all time, including the Master himself, Sir Donald Bradman, it, was, in fact, a bowler who first imprinted the name of Australia on the cricket world's consciousness. He was the first of the modern bowlers, who studied the game with an intensity which was in itself frightening. He was tall – over 6 ft 2 in. – but thin, as he weighed only eleven stone; and after he had bowled out England at The Oval in 1882 men called him "The Demon".

Frederick Robert Spofforth was born in 1855. In his own words he has told how he started bowling and how he developed his action:

"When I was a boy at school, at the Glebe, near Sydney, I used to bowl underhand, as nearly everybody did at that time in Australia. It was very fast – almost as fast as my round* – and generally a good length. Then an English team came over in '62 or '63 and, of course, their bowlers had adopted the new system. I watched this carefully and came to the conclusion that the way to bowl like the Englishmen was to throw. So I diligently practised, until I became quite an expert at this, and very fast. I met with considerable success, too, for although it was explained to me that I had missed the idea, I felt sure I was right, and the umpires contented themselves with hinting a doubt.

"Two gentlemen, named Kelly and Read, were not satisfied with merely telling me that I was not doing the proper thing, but showed me what to do, and I at once set to work to bowl round. I left the Glebe and went to Eglington College, where there were about 200 boys, and while

*By which he means roundarm.

42

there played for two first-class clubs, Newton and the Albert. In '72 or '73 I played against W. G. Grace's team. Afterwards, I went to the English and Scottish Bank at Sydney and then to the New South Wales Bank, playing cricket on Saturdays.

"I thought it (his style) over for a long time. When I saw Tarrant (in 1864), who was the fastest bowler I ever knew, I tried to copy him. My one aim was to bowl as fast as possible, without any other idea at all. But when Southerton and Alfred Shaw came (ten years later) their bowling was a revelation, and I didn't see any reason why I shouldn't copy them as well as Tarrant, and try to combine all three. I very soon found that variation in pace was the most important thing of all, and with the object of disguising it I tried various experiments until I gradually found what seemed to me a style which was the best for disguise as well as for ease.

"People used to say 'Look how he bends down when he delivers the ball; it must take it out of him immensely.' But that bend was just the thing that prevented any strain. As an illustration of this, you sometimes see little boys throwing a piece of clay from the end of a stick. What sort of a stick do they choose? It is one that bends easily. You will notice that the clay cannot be sent half as far from a rigid stick, or half as easily. When a boxer hits out from the shoulder, you don't see him stand bolt upright; he leans forward as he hits, and so avoids the jar which he must otherwise feel. In bowling you will invariably find that a man who delivers a very fast ball with an upright action can only bowl well for a few overs, after which the shock which he feels every time he puts his foot down is altogether too much for him, and he bowls without the same fire."

This carefully worked-out style and relentless determination brought him 1146 wickets at 13.55 each in first-class cricket, including 14 wickets for 90 in the famous Oval Test which created the Ashes series. George Giffen, another "great" who played in that match with him, reported with a mixture of awe and *lèse majesté*: "I remember on our way to England in 1882, Spoff had figured in a fancy-dress ball as Mephistopheles; but, aided by art, he did not look half the demon he did when at The Oval on that Tuesday afternoon he sent in those marvellous breaks, every one of which, if it had passed the bat, would have hit the wicket.

"One gentleman in the pavilion is said to have remarked, 'If they would only play with straight bats then they would be sure to get the runs.' To which his companion, a lady, replied 'Would they really? Couldn't you get them some?'

"But their failure was pardonable. If W. G. had been at one end and Murdoch the other (the rival captains) Spofforth might have been

43

beaten, but I doubt it. Irresistible as an avalanche, he had bowled his last 11 overs for two runs and four wickets. The finest piece of bowling I have ever seen!"

Once again, it seems worthwhile to give a few statistics, to stand up the eulogy with fact. *Wisden Cricketers' Almanack* carried them in 1927:

10 for 20 (including hat-trick) Australians v MCC; Lord's 1878

9 for 53 Australians v Lancashire; Manchester 1878

13 for 110 (including hat-trick) Australia v England; Melbourne 1878

13 for 85 Australians v Derbyshire, 1880

9 for 51 and 4 for 34 Australians v Somerset, 1882

14 for 90 Australia v England; The Oval, 1882

8 for 11 and 6 for 47 Australians v Scotland, 1882

7 for 3 and 7 for 34 Australians v An England XI, 1884

13 for 123 Australians v Players, 1884

14 for 96 Australians v Players, 1884

7 for 16 Australians v Middlesex, 1884

13 for 85 Australians v Cambridge U past and Present, 1884

15 for 36 Australians v Oxford U, 1886

7 for 19 Australians v North of England, 1886

15 for 81 Australians v Derbyshire, 1889

9 for 56 and 5 for 58 Derbyshire v Leicestershire, 1890

8 for 74 MCC v Yorkshire, 1896

In England Spofforth took 9 wickets in 20 balls against Eighteen of Hastings in 1878 and in a match in 1880 he took 12 wickets in 18 balls.

In 1888 Spofforth decided to live permanently in Britain – at least he gave himself six months to find success. He joined the office of the Star Tea Company in Derbyshire as a clerk, and within six months was general manager. He turned out a fine business man, became a director and eventually chairman, and when he died he left £164,000.

S. M. J. Woods, describing the famous Spofforth action, said when he bowled he looked "all arms, legs and nose" and he had "more guile than any bowler I saw; a perfect followthrough, and he delivered every ball with the same action, so it was hard to distinguish what ball was coming next." C. B. Fry reasoned that "I formed the useful guiding principle that even a demon on an evil wicket could only bowl one ball at a time, and if you really look at the ball you have a good chance of playing it." And the Hon. Ivo Bligh, who led one of the first victorious English sides in Australia, and later became Lord Darnley, wrote: "The long arms seemed to be whirling round at much the same speed whether the ball was coming fast or slow, and he had practised these disguises to perfection. He was incomparably the best stayer of any fast or medium-paced bowler I can remember. No bowler I ever saw had a more graceful, spacious sweep of the arm, and his delivery gave a most satisfactory sensation of perfection of pace and power combined." His conclusion: "One of the very best bowlers the past 50 years have seen, unquestionably; possibly the best of all."

And W. G. Grace, the champion batsman, wrote in his *Cricketing Reminiscences and Personal Recollections:* "He was unique as a fast bowler, and practically established a school of bowlers. His pace was terrifically fast at times, his length excellent, and his breakbacks exceedingly deceptive. He controlled the ball with masterly skill, and if the wicket helped him ever so little, he was virtually unplayable. A good many batsmen funked Spofforth's bowling, and a great many more found it impossible to score off him."

Spofforth was a forthright man with ideas that he had worked out for himself which often ran counter to the established way of thinking, and he had a totally clear view of his own performance. He admitted that his staggering performance on his first visit to England, at Lord's, had a great deal to do with his losing his temper with an unnamed clergyman who wondered what these "niggers" could do. In fact, he was no mean psychologist in his methods.

'At Lord's on May 27, 1878, Spofforth took 10 wickets for 20 runs in his first match in England, obtaining the hat-trick against a very strong side including W. G. Grace and A. N. Hornby, ("Oh, my Hornby and my Barlow long ago"). MCC were dismissed for 33 and 19, being beaten in a single day by an innings.

Spofforth,* in his later years, answered the comment that his performance in that match had caused great astonishment in England:

"Perhaps there was," he said. "But that was only because I was an Australian bowler. If an Englishman had done the same thing against the same team on that wicket, you wouldn't have been in the least surprised. You must remember that we were hardly understood at first – in fact it is well known that a clergyman was astonished to find we were not black.

"The fact is I varied my pace a great deal, which was not the rule at that time. Moreover, the wicket suited me and I came back a lot. I think surprise had very much to do with the result. I used to put mid-on almost close to the batsman, and this had a discouraging effect. At that time I could trust myself not to bowl a ball which might be dangerous to my mid-on, and he could trust me too. No-one was ever hurt there, but, of course, unless a man was a wonderful fielder he did

*This conversation is summarised from *Chats on the Cricket Field* by W. A. Bettesworth, an old-timer who would talk for hours to anyone and then set it all down for a doting public

The Demon. F. R. Spofforth, who first won the "Ashes" for his country.

Jack Gregory – "an awe-inspiring spectacle".

A century of Australian thunderbolts.

Ray Lindwall – smooth, brilliantly accurate. A superb athlete in action.

Jeff Thomson. Mean, moody, magnificent "slinger" at 100 mph.

not get there."

"When you were at the height of your success, did you ever find the crowd at all hostile to you?"

"Quite the contrary. They often mobbed me, but only in the friendliest way. When we beat England at The Oval by seven runs, I was carried into the pavilion, which I reached almost without a shirt on my back; but it was anything but hostility which caused this.

"Once, however, we were playing at Keighley, in Yorkshire, on a bumpy wicket, I'm afraid I was bowling very fast indeed, and was knocking men about a little – *a fast bowler has to frighten a batsman sometimes.* (MY italics.) Suddenly an old Yorkshireman rose up among the crowd and, amid a dead silence, called out in his loudest tones, 'Chain t'long beggar up; he's trying to kill 'em.'

"At Sheffield, the crowd got over the ropes and took up a lot of space. I was in the long-field, and it was often difficult to move. A ball had been hit in my direction, and the people showed no disposition to let me go by, when a Sheffielder constituted himself spokesman, and yelled out 'Mak' way for'm lads – let t'old demon have a chance.' They made way at once in the most docile manner."

Finally, Spofforth had this advice to all future fast bowlers which, today, might well be taken to heart in England, where desperate searches have been going on all over the country to "find a fast bowler" to fill the gap which has existed in English cricket since Trueman Statham and Snow:

"Have you any theory as to the way in which a boy should learn to bowl, Mr Spofforth?"

"I have: but I am quite aware that it is heresy, for it is entirely opposed to the advice given in books. A boy is always told to begin by bowling slow, but I am convinced he ought to do just the opposite. You will understand, of course, that I do not mean that he should always bowl fast, or that he should strain himself in the slightest degree. But he should, within his strength, learn how to bowl fast, and to increase his pace every year. In this way he will have something to vary from, the variation is almost everything. I am certain that it is very much better to vary the pace from a fast ball than from a slow.

"Strength has very little to do with fast bowling. Everything depends on the elasticity of the arm. The reason why so many boys and men overblow themselves is not because they bowl too fast, but because they don't do it in a rational manner, and keep on their top speed without variation. The only thing they should be taught is not to use all their force, but to bowl fast by allowing their joints to work quite freely."

Well, Ernest Jones, Ted McDonald, Stan McCabe, Ray Lindwall, Alan Davidson and Dennis Lillee in a distinguished line (not to omit

48

Gubby Allen, Ken Farnes, Brian Statham, Frank Tyson, Freddie Trueman and John Snow; or Learie Constantine, Wesley Hall, Garfield Sobers, Andy Roberts and Michael Holding; or Peter Heine, Peter Pollock and Mike Proctor; or Sarfraz Nawaz to name but a random few) have been following the great man's advice for a century now, with, one must admit, some pretty fair results.

Incidentally, compare the pictures, taken a century apart, of Spofforth as he delivered the ball; and Sarfraz. If ever a style has been handed down, it is there for all to see.

As Cardus said, he brought bowling under the control of the mind.

*   *   *   *   *

Spofforth, of course, was not the only Australian gift to the Golden Age. There was his partner, Harry Boyle, the first "silly mid-on" who aided and abetted Spoff by snapping up the close catches somewhere near the batsman's hip pocket. The position became known as "Boyley's mid-on".

In his own right Boyle was a great bowler too, medium-paced, who, like Sydney Barnes later, could spin the ball either way. He was a master of length, had a deceptive flight, and could take punishment. But for all a plethora of good figures, he was still the junior partner.

George Eugene Palmer succeeded him as Spofforth's "chief assistant", another medium-pace spinner. George Giffen, one of the real characters in the game, reckoned him Australia's finest in the 'eighties. He added Spofforth's yorker to his equipment, but he played for only seven years, losing his skill and pace owing to too much experiment with leg-spinners and also to a knee injury. But he made four trips to England in that time, and took 78 English wickets in seventeen Tests at 21.51 apiece.

Spofforth, incidentally, for all his imposing manner, could, and did, tell the most outrageous stories with an utterly straight face, according to his grand-daughter, Miss Pamela Spofforth, now one of Britain's leading coaches of the violin. The late C. I. Thornton told one of them in *Wisden*: "How did you become such a fine slip fielder?" he asked, and Spofforth replied, gravely: "When I was young I made a boy throw stones into a hedge, and as the sparrows flew out, I caught them."

His place as the master was taken by Charles Turner, yet another medium-pace bowler of the Spofforth school, but with his own brand of genius. A. C. MacLaren, himself a majestic opening bat for England, described him as "all life as he walked back when, with a sudden swing around, he would come tripplingly to the wicket in the most cheery and, at the same time, graceful manner possible. His action was perfect, likewise his length, and he put heart and soul into every ball he bowled." His action was more "square-on" than most great bowlers, none of the "left shoulder towards the batsman". His partner was a sprightly left-hander, Jack Ferris. They did two tours of England together, and the story of their quite amazing deeds is told in figures.

1888	Overs	Maidens	Runs	Wickets	Average
Turner	2589.3	1222	3492	314	11.12
Ferris	2222.2	998	3101	220	14.10
1890					
Turner	1651.1	724	2755	215	12.60
Ferris	1685.4	688	2838	215	13.20

In 1888 eleven others shared the rest of the bowling, taking 129 wickets between them. In 1890 five others bowled and took 167 wickets.

Hugh Trumble, said C. B. Fry, was a bowler "in every way worthy of the great Australian traditions. Not only does he have a perfect command over the ball, but knows every jot and tittle of the art of bowling. His wisdom and knowledge is cricket and proverbial among cricketers. He is very tall, and delivers the ball with his arm high above his head, so he can make the ball nip upwards from the pitch. His mastery of length is perfect. On good wickets he relies on his length and change of pace to get batsmen out, though he can generally make the ball do a little both ways. On anything like a bowler's wicket he is almost unplayable; his off-break is absolutely deadly, and he makes judicious use of the plain straight ball."

Trumble was also one of the first bowlers to play on the batsman's strength rather than his weaknesses. A good driver, for example, would be "fed" half-volleys outside the off stump, hitting fours and stinging the packed cover field's hands, until a subtle change of pace and length would cause the ball to be lifted into someone's hands.

He was a genial giant, with a fund of stories. He told Bettesworth: "I was once playing at Hay, in New South Wales, against a team composed of squatters, one of whom had driven sixty miles to the match. It seems that he had made the bet with another of his side as to who would get the bigger score. To make matters sure, he came up to us and, after finding out who was going to bowl, told us that if we would let him break his duck he would bring us a live emu, while if we let him get half a dozen he would bring a live white kangaroo. We determined to let him get some runs just to see what sort of stock he raised in that part of the world; but the man with whom he had made the bet was too sharp for him. *He* squared the umpire, and got one of our team to promise to appeal first ball when his rival was in. We didn't know that, of course, and so the first ball was a short one, wide of the wicket.

The batsman missed it, there was a shout of 'How's that?' and the umpire promptly replied 'Out!' So we didn't get our white kangaroo."

In 1896, Ernest Jones – "Jonah" to friend and foe alike – made his first tour of England. He started by taking the wickets of Grace, Fry, Jackson, Ranji, Shrewsbury, William Gunn and another for 84 runs. Jackson, the great F. S., had two ribs broken, one ball flew through Grace's beard ("Sorry, Doc, she slipped") and only Ranjitsinhji, who was a magician anyway, could counter the terrific speed. He flicked the ball off his eyebrows as though he was swatting flies, and scored a brilliant 80. Ranji often described Jones as a "slinger", not because he was so fast. There apparently was some suspicion that he might have thrown the occasional ball, but generally the umpires were satisfied.

Fry said Jones was the fastest bowler who had ever represented Australia. "Indeed, for a few overs he is probably the fastest bowler there has ever been. The main element of his success is, of course, his great pace. He very rarely bowls a bad-length ball, and is quite free of the tendency so common in fast bowlers of giving the batsman a chance of the leg side. He keeps the ball on and just outside the off stump; sometimes it keeps straight, but now and then it comes back enough to beat the bat. He takes a run of a moderate length, and pounds the ball into the ground with every ounce of strength he has. He is extremely powerful, and the ball leaves a mark on the hardest wicket. He is an indefatigable worker."

He was the first Australian express.

*　　*　　*　　*　　*

Bowling, of course, was not all the Australians had to offer the Golden Age. There was Victor Trumper, the supreme stylist of that or any other age; Clem Hill, who set new standards of batsmanship for left-handers; M. A. Noble, the first of the really great captains (after W. G.); George Giffen, all-rounder extraordinary; Alec Bannerman, after Scotton the original "barn-door"; John McCarthy Blackham, the wicket-keeper who stood up to "Spoff"; and a gentleman named Percy Stanislaus McDonnell, who died when he was 36. "One of the very best and jolliest players," wrote Giffen. ". . . it was when things were going wrong that he was seen at his best. Maybe at times he would let fly in a dangerously desperate style, but if he stayed, didn't he just warm up the off-theory! . . . . I saw him compile 124 and 83 in a Test match at Adelaide, and if I live to be a hundred I shall not see more elegant, graceful and effective batting. If 'hit' was the game he would blaze away like fury, but if he were not under orders and the wicket were good, he would settle down and bat as prettily as Palairet. At Adelaide his was the poetry of batting." A stylist indeed.

Victor Trumper was undoubtedly the paragon, the fairest flower of the Australian crop of the Golden Age. If W. G. had been all majesty and grandeur and Ranji all Oriental witchcraft, Trumper brought to cricket a sunlit magic all of his own. No batsman in the long story of cricket could so captivate the crowd and slaughter an attack at the same time, all done with exquisite grace, twinkling footwork and effortless timing. His best year was in England in 1902, wet and desolate summer that was the despair of many a batsman. Trumper made 2570 runs, more than any other English or Australian batsman.

Some cricketers may be judged by statistics, wrote A. A. Thomson; some by eccentricity and some by massive achievement. A rare and enchanted few are remembered for the sheer beauty they brought to the game. Trumper, they used to say, had several strokes for every ball; a vivid fielder and a personality of commanding charm. The cricketer's Bible, *Wisden Cricketers' Almanack*, is not given to high-flown phrases; it never has been; and its virtue lies as much in its sobriety as its accuracy and the interminability of its records. Yet even *Wisden* let its hair down about Trumper:

"No-one has been at once so brilliant and so consistent since W. G. was at his best. . . . He seemed independent of varying conditions, being able to play just as dazzling a game after a night's rain as when the wickets were hard and true. All bowling came alike to him . . . in the Tests at Sheffield and Manchester he reduced our best bowlers to the level of the village green . . . the way in which he took good-length balls off the middle stump and sent them to the boundary had to be seen to be believed . . . for the moment he is unapproachable."

The batsmen who would not approach him included Shrewsbury, Ranjitsinhji, Abel, Grace, R. E. Foster, Fry, Jessop, Jackson, MacLaren, Warner, Palairet and Hayward. And the bowlers he reduced to village green trundlers were Hirst, Rhodes, Braund, Barnes, Jackson, Lockwood, Cranfield, Trott and Tate. In 1902 those nine bowlers took over 1200 wickets between them, and Trumper, said Thomson, just felt sorry for them.

For a little while, B. J. T. Bosanquet worried Trumper with the googly, as Mailey said, but only for a while; and he flayed Bosanquet and his great South African disciples on scores of later occasions. He was so quick on his feet, tripping one-two, one-two down the wicket as if in his own *"chassée"*, to get to the pitch of the ball; in his own words, once you got there it didn't matter which way the ball turned. He was slightly built but his timing was such that he hit with tremendous power, and of all the batsmen of his day only Jessop could match his brilliance. When he died in 1915 after an illness had cut short his career, the news took the war off the front pages for a day, and people

52

lined the streets of Sydney six-deep to watch his funeral. Eleven crick-eters carried his coffin. In spite of all the deeds of Don Bradman, there are still older cricketers, not only Australians, who regard Victor Trumper as the finest batsman their country has ever produced.

Alexander Bannerman, one of the first of the stonewallers, would have been proud in later years to see Trevor Bailey, Jackie McGlew and Bill Lawry in action. He would have known that the virtues of a stout heart and a straight bat were still valued, 80 or so years later. But, said Giffen, he was something more than a mere stonewaller, for when the opportunity came he could hit the ball very hard. He used always to watch for a loose one to leg in the first over in an innings, or when a new bowler was put on, and he often hit three fours in an over and then retired into imperturbability for another half-hour without scoring a run. Often he pulled Australia out of a hole, plodding along at one end while wickets tumbled at the other, unnoticed almost except by the fielding side, whose patience he sorely tried.

George Giffen leaves behind this vivid account of a Bannerman innings, of which latter-day slow-coaches would have been proud. It saved the match and won the rubber for Australia in 1892, when Jack Blackham was the Australian captain.

"The next day rain fell, and the innings closed at 391. Alec Banner-man was responsible for the odd 91. I shall never forget the sight of the field crowded round him as he stonewalled. There was W. G. at point, almost on the point of his bat; Lohmann a couple of yards away at slip; Peel at silly point; Stoddart only a dozen yards away at mid-off; and Briggs at silly mid-on. One gentleman remarked that it reminded him of a famous painting, *Anguish,* in which a bevy of crows are swarming over a dead lamb, over which the mother is watching. A barracker cal-led out: 'Look out Alec, or W. G. will have his hand in your pocket.' But Alec stonewalled on, imperturbably blocking the straight ones, sardonically smiling at the off-theory, and judiciously tapping a loose one to leg, suddenly he swished at an off-ball and cut it past W. G.'s ear to the boundary. What a yell rent the air! He was eventually caught by W. G. off Briggs, who simply tossed the balls down slowly, with as much twizzle as possible on them, in the hope that he might lead Alec into an indiscretion. But the Englishmen had to wait seven and a half hours for that indiscretion! Truly, patience is a virtue."

Sometimes his colleagues felt that his keenness had developed into over-seriousness. George Giffen recalled the time when a young ass of a slip fielder whiled away the time between overs singing snatches of music-hall ditties. Alec Bannerman stood it for a while. Eventually he marched up to the young man and, with the sternness of a judge sen-tencing a murderer to death, delivered his verdict: "Do you know, my

After "Stonewall" Jackson, came A. C. Bannerman, early Australian rock.

friend, you are playing cricket? If you want to play cricket, play it; and if you want to sing, go and sing, but for Heaven's sake don't sing comic songs in the slips!"

The story reminds me of a ticking-off I overheard at Old Trafford only last summer, when some youngsters behind the member's stand were indulging in that most modern of cricket's abuses, banging tin cans together with dull and repetitive rhythm. A middle-aged man in shirtsleeves, with a red face and greying, receding hair, told them to stop it. They persisted. He turned on them, and in a rich Lancashire accent, embellished liberally with four-letter words, he told them: "If you don't shut up this moment, you'll be out of the ground and down the police station. You're in a cricket ground, and when you're in a cricket ground you have to be a gentleman, or at least behave like one. So bloody shut up, or else I'll come down off this stand and kick your arse from here to next Tuesday."

He was so emphatic, so obviously meant what he said, but I wondered, in 1978, whether there was any chance of its working. It did. No more tin cans were clattered in that part of the ground for the whole five days of the Test match.

Clement Hill, the forerunner of so many great Australian left-hand batsmen, first toured England in 1896, when he was 19. He was short, quick, and possessed a fine defence. "He watches the ball very carefully, is extremely quick with his bat and on his feet, and always plays absolutely straight," said Fry. "He holds his bat with one hand at the top and one at the bottom of the handle and stands crouching ever so little, with his knees slightly bent. He gets most of his runs by extremely skilful placing on the on side and to leg; his power of forcing straight balls in these directions is remarkable. He cuts safely in a manner peculiar to himself, has a nice pushing off-drive, and can hit low and hard over the bowler's or mid-on's head. He can hook a short ball round to the on side with certainty even on a fast wicket. He has strong wrists, and often scores even when playing back."

Close your eyes, forget the name Hill, open them and read that passage again, substituting John Edrich, whose hundredth hundred in first-class cricket arrived in 1977.

★ ★ ★ ★ ★

In the years before the First World War Australian cricket was distinguished from that of England largely by the quality of its leaders, and I think it would not be too strong to say that it was in this department of the game that Australia was more often than not vastly superior. With such a vast array of talent at her command, it really was extraordinary that England *lost* so many Test matches. The great England captain of the era was reckoned to be Archie MacLaren, skipper of Lancashire, and my father's idol as a schoolboy. I recall being most severely rebuked for suggesting that MacLaren had indeed set a style of his own – he captained England in four series against Australia, and lost the lot!

M. A. Noble was the man who set the stamp of greatness on the captaincy of Australia. He succeeded Joe Darling, left-hand bat and everybody's favourite, loved and admired by everyone who played under him. But Noble excelled him in shrewdness, tactical knowledge and enormous authority of character.

Tall, powerful in build, and with the large nose that stands for strength of character (remember Spofforth?), he was a fighter, a martinet on the field, determined in his own play, and almost puritanical in his belief in the principles of cricket – not merely in the batting, bowling, and fielding but in comportment on the field of play.

He had all the necessary talents with which to lead from the front, setting his players no task that he couldn't perform himself. He could fit either into the bowling or batting picture, and was a fine fielder at point. He was a graceful and effective batsman, with a classic style, a strong drive, an immaculate cut, and a wristy leg glance. His main asset as a bowler was his deceptive flight. But he brought more than these attributes to his task – he made a study and a science of field placement so as to save runs. It was a science in which in latter years Don Bradman graduated with the highest honours, but Noble had worked out most of the tricks in advance.

He never forgot the lesson he learnt (and for which he was criticised quite sharply at the time) when R. E. Foster hit 287 against Australia, but in later years his field was as impassable as a rabbit-proof fence. Woe betide a fieldsman who strayed from the exact position in which he'd been placed with mathematical accuracy. Noble always believed a cricketer should think, should realise that he was part of a team, and should obey his leader implicitly. He could not tolerate slackness of any kind. Rolling a ball along the ground to the bowler, instead of throwing it through the air, would bring down the wrath of Jehovah. The late A. G. Moyes, to whom I am indebted for these notes, recorded that Noble would get furious if a batsman picked up the ball for the bowler or fielder. "Your job is to bat. Let others do the fielding," he would say tersely.

"He was the last of the line which was the backbone of the Australian attack from the days of Spofforth onward," wrote Moyes. Noble had a fairly long run to the wicket, with the ball hidden in his ample fingers, and arm swinging freely at his side as he advanced to the crease. He was, of course, an off-spinner, had all the virtues of length

56

and control, but added to them some curious features which made his bowling different. He could bowl a genuine swerve – and it was distinct from the swing which takes effect as the ball leaves the bowler's hand and curves its way down the pitch. Noble used spin, and his slower one would drop away late, after the batsman had gone into his stroke and could not retreat. It was a nasty ball, difficult to follow, and even more difficult to counter, especially when bowled into a stiff breeze which gave the wind resistance and helped the bowler in his art."

But it was as a captain, a student of and developer of theories of attack and defence, that his major contribution to the game was made.

Warwick Armstrong weighed eight stone when he first played for Australia in 1902; and twenty stone when he finished as captain of the post-war sides nineteen years later. In between he was an orthodox leg-spinner who could bowl for hours on a length, and even turn the ball up the Lord's slope if he had a wicket which suited him. It was under his leadership that Australia slaughtered England in the first post-war Tests, using a brand new weapon: all-out speed with two complementary fast bowlers. But this is getting ahead of the story, for cricket had also taken root in South Africa and had flourished vigorously from the start, with speed, and spin, and a great batsman or two to set the standards which began high and prospered until politics took so many high-class players out of the international scene for good.

South Africa was the third nation to enter into the international arena. The first South African side to visit England came in 1894, and Lord Hawke took teams from England in 1895–96 and 1897–98. Matches against Australia began in 1902.

The players who first made their mark for South Africa were J. H. Sinclair, a hard-hitting batsman who made the country's first century; and J. J. Kotze, for 50 years the fastest bowler South Africa produced until Neil Adcock.

But South African cricket's own Golden Age owed its coming to that remarkable innovator, B. J. T. Bosanquet. G. A. Faulkner, A. E. E. Vogler and G. C. White adopted the style, and in 1907 they won 21 of their 31 matches and drew two Tests, losing the third.

The most gifted, and the man who disguised the "wrong 'un" best was Vogler, who in 1909–10 in South Africa took 36 wickets in a Test series against England. By common consent, though, Aubrey Faulkner was one of the greatest cricketers to come from South Africa. His career resembled that of Rhodes. In his early days he was more bowler than batsman; for many years he bore comparison with the best as an all-rounder; and when his bowling deserted him he charmed spectators and opponents all over the world with his batting. He batted magnificently on tour in Australia in 1911–12, scoring 732 runs in the Tests with an average of 73.20; only Trumper, then at the height of his powers could compare with him.

Herby Taylor was South Africa's greatest batsman, after Faulkner, in the first quarter-century. He had a delightfully correct style, feet always in the right place, good balance, immaculate technique. Most of his runs came in front of the wicket, and many of his best strokes were played off the back foot. His duels with S. F. Barnes became a feature of the 1913–14 tour, in which Barnes took 49 wickets in only four Test matches. Taylor was the only batsman who could play him, and he played innings of 109, 70, 93 and 87 in the tests, and 100, 91 and 83 not out in provincial matches.

"Dave" Nourse was also a prominent figure, if a dour and defensive one, in the years before the first war. But his deeds were far surpassed by his son, Dudley, who hit 231 – at that time South Africa's highest score – against Australia in the second Test at Johannesburg in the 1935–36 tour. Dudley inherited his father's skill, dourness and temperament for the big occasion, but he was altogether a more attractive and polished batsman. He was stocky, broad-shouldered and with extremely strong forearms which enabled him to hit with stunning force off the back foot.

He was fortunate, too, in batting in the same side as Alan Melville and Bruce Mitchell, two further names to conjure with. Melville started his cricket in South Africa, developed it in England to captain Oxford University, then captained South Africa and became the first South African to hit a century in each innings of a Test match (recovering from a broken finger and limping with an injured thigh). He captained his country in the marathon Test in Durban in 1939 – the one that never ended – and he scored a century in that too. He was 6 ft 2 in. tall, had a splendid array of strokes, was classical in style, with perfect timing on the leg side. He was an admirable leader of rare courage.

Bruce Mitchell was South Africa's nearest equivalent to Sir Leonard Hutton, although in his later years he sometimes carried caution to extremes. The culminating point in his career arrived in 1947, when at The Oval he was on the field for the whole of the five days, less fifteen minutes, batting in all for 13 hours 20 minutes, making 120 in the first innings and 189 not out in the second. Like Melville, he was stylish and powerful, with very good defence and inexhaustible patience.

58

3
Between the Wars

The two great punctuation-marks of the twentieth century, the world wars, form convenient breathing spaces for any surveyor of the human scene. Cricket, the most civilised sport of all, like civilisation itself, staggered, faltered and then, all but mortally wounded, paused for breath and fought its way back to life and vigour. Many cricketers lost their lives, and for many more the gaps of four and six years were fatal to their careers. English cricket on both occasions suffered more than that in the rest of the world, just as England herself was more badly affected than any of the rest of the cricket-playing world.

But as we have already noted, a number of players did survive to straddle both pre- and post-war periods; and cricket recovered to blossom again in the 'twenties and 'thirties, to produce stars of the magnitude of Walter Hammond, Stan McCabe, Hedley Verity and Bill O'Reilly. Overshadowing them all, of course, was Don Bradman, the compact, determined and utterly ruthless Australian who was the greatest run-gatherer of all.

England, worse hit as we have said, still began after the First World War with Rhodes, Barnes, J. W. H. T. Douglas, George Gunn, Herbert Strudwick, and most important of all, another small, compact figure in one J. B. Hobbs, of Surrey. All these men had played Test cricket before the war; as had Warwick Armstrong and one other figure whom we have seen before, and who had a whole array of individual talents under one skin – Charles Macartney.

By far the most interesting figures of the early 'twenties were Hobbs and Macartney, both magnificent batsmen with individual styles as different from each other as Gorgonzola cheese is from Double Gloucester. Continuing our theme, perhaps it is fair to say that Macartney was in direct line of descent from the electric Trumper and Jessop, while Hobbs inherited (via Tom Hayward, the man who coached him) his style, his inevitability, his all-round-the-wicket shots, from Grace way back and, much closer, from C. B. Fry. Macartney had started before the war as an all-rounder – slow left-arm bowler and punishing right-hand batsman. At Birmingham in 1909 he bowled MacLaren and Fry and had Hobbs l.b.w. for a total of 5 runs; and at Leeds in the same rubber he took 11 wickets for 85 runs. And even after the war, in 1921, with Warwick Armstrong's all-conquering team, he took 8 Leicestershire wickets for 41 in a total of 136; then he proceeded to score 50 runs in half an hour and 177 in all. On the same tour, he hit 345 against Nottingham in *just under 4 hours*. When he'd made 9 George Gunn missed him in the slips, and said afterwards: "They should have started a collection for me." In mid-afternoon A. W. Carr, the Notts captain, decided to "make a move". He changed his bowlers round. "I did it just to let the high hats in the pavilion know that I hadn't lost control of the situation." Carr decided to bowl the over to enable the change of ends to be made. "I thought it would look well in the scorebook: A. W. Carr one over one maiden no runs no wickets."

The scorebook actually read 1–0–24–0.

And the unfortunate Carr also missed Macartney at 2 on the day he scored a century before lunch at Leeds in July 1926 after Carr, by then captain of England, had won the toss and put Australia in to bat.

Sir Neville Cardus regarded "The Governor-General", as he was called in Australia, more highly even than Bradman, whom he was inclined to dismiss as a mere run-machine.

"In style he was a sort of Bradman de luxe, Bradman plus wit and genius for improvisation. When Bradman was scoring at his fastest, his cricket seemed pre-organised, so to say, every stroke planned and perfectly executed accordingly. Macartney's batting gave the impression that it was perpetually creative throughout an innings, with several strokes for the same kind of ball. He was, like Sir Donald, a killer, ruthless in attack. But his style and presence told us that he was vastly enjoying himself, especially when, at the last split second, he changed an incipient off-drive into a late-cut.

"Even the most attractive players occasionally disappoint and bore us on days when they are 'out of touch'. Macartney was never uninteresting; when he had to suffer one of those dull fallible moods which come inexplicably over the greatest, he got out."

He was always confident, aggressive in his batting, but never conceited. When Cardus asked him once how he would compare himself with Trumper, he replied: "I'd always have been proud to carry his cricket bag." And another of his sayings is worth commending to today's parade of cowed batsmen: "Any batsman worth his salt," he said, "should let the bowlers understand at once that he is the boss here today."

How many, indeed, can or even endeavour to follow that advice? Vivian Richards, Barry Richards, Procter once in a while, Greig once in a

60

blue moon and, until he became captain of Australia, Greg Chappell used to; perhaps also Majid Khan and Zaheer Abbas.

Warwick Armstrong's teams in 1921 were probably the best-balanced, strongest and most successful until the Bradman era dawned some eight years later. Armstrong, allying his sturdy batting to his bowling, topped the batting averages himself, and he had Oldfield, the redoubtable wicketkeeper, Mailey, the first of Australia's great between-war spinners, and above all Jack Gregory and Ted McDonald, the first genuine pair of speed merchants used together by any country as their open attack.

These days, it is customary to hear commentators say, "Of course, fast bowlers have always been most successful when operating in pairs." Warwick Armstrong set the style in 1921, Gregory and McDonald were the operators, and England were the victims (which also set something of a style).

Jack Gregory was the senior partner, hugely-built, several inches over six feet tall. There is a marvellously evocative description of his bowling action by A. C. MacLaren in *Cricket, Old and New*. "... And Gregory does run terribly. Nature has provided him with the most thoroughly adequate feet for the purpose, and he makes the most of them. He employs his face also to add to the dismay his approach is calculated to inspire. In repose his face is pleasant enough, but when he is making haste to hurl the ball in the direction of a fellow creature whose only offence is to be armed with a bat and some pads, it becomes the kind of face one would not like a nervous child to see just before going to bed. With those great pounding feet, the great whirling arms, and the face, he is indeed an awe-inspiring spectacle."

More factually, Moyes described how Gregory took a very long run starting with a shuffle of the feet like the boxer rubbing his boots in the resin, and then moved his fourteen stone forward like an avalanche (though faster) increasing his speed until he gathered full momentum, finishing with a huge bound of some nine feet as he let loose his thunderbolts. His action was not without rhythm, but it lacked the charm of McDonald's because he gained his speed from strength rather than from smooth efficiency. But the strength was there to urge the flying ball, which he brought down from a stupendous height, making it lift chest-high from a good length, sometimes away from the bat, sometimes across the body according to the direction of the wind.

If the batsman was fortunate or skilful enough to move to the other end he had no respite. There was Ted McDonald, also over six feet tall, with dark hair that flopped over his eyes as he bowled. His action was all poetry – smooth, rhythmical, a gliding motion, effortless and sinewy, disguising the speed – an earlier Holding. His arms worked in unison with his legs and body; then with a windmill action he would bring his right arm over so high that it brushed against his ear. When flat out he could make the ball fly head-high, using the cocked wrist to add that little extra flick as he delivered the ball. In eight Tests in which they opened together, they took 61 wickets between them. If McDonald was the Statham of the pair, Gregory was the Trueman; or another projection might find Lindwall and Miller, or Hall and Griffith, or Holding and Daniel.

The Gregory-McDonald combination was a break from the tradition that variety was the spice of life, that you used a fast man with a slow, a left-hander with a right-hander. They made history, and set a pattern for the future which would bring the crowds flocking in to cricket grounds all over the world. Millions went to see Bradman bat, and Hammond and Compton and the three Ws for West Indies. But since 1921 what has set the hearts thumping and the turnstiles rattling more than anything else has been the prospect of two great fast bowlers in full cry, battering down an innings by force and thunder and shock. It's primitive, I know, and there lurks in this breast, at least, a longing to see a batsman, in the 'seventies, do what Stan McCabe did to the most fearsome attack of all, the Larwood bodyline blitz in 1932.

McCabe was only 22 at the time, Bradman was missing from the team through illness, and 82 runs were scored for 3 wickets at Sydney when McCabe came to the wicket. More about bodyline later; suffice to say that it was lightning fast, short, and directed at the batsman's body and head with the express intention to intimidate him. In three hours that day McCabe hit 127 before the close, and the next morning he added 60 more while 4 batsmen fell the other end adding 10 runs. He stood up to the battering unflinchingly, hooked and hooked and hooked again the bouncers streaming at his head; and when he tired of that he stepped *back*, away from the wicket, and *cut* them past the slips from behind the leg stump, as Jessop used to do.

(I have seen it happen once, actually; not in a first-class match, but in the Australia v West Indies one-day Test in the Prudential World Cup match of 1975, when Alvin Kallicharran, the tiny West Indian left-hander, smashed Dennis Lillee for 34 off 10 balls and won the match.)

Gregory faded out of Test cricket in 1928, but McDonald went to England and became Lancashire's number one bowler, particularly in 1928 and 1929, when they won the Championship. His duels with Larwood were legends in themselves, coupled with his duels with George Gunn, one of the finest players of fast bowling of his day.

At Old Trafford, one evening after rain on hard ground, reported Cardus, Larwood made the ball fly alarmingly. One or two Lancashire

62

caps, sporting the red rose, were knocked flying. Next morning McDonald went into the Notts dressing-room and told them to ring up the Royal Infirmary and order a "few" stretchers. He then proceeded to bombard the Nottinghamshire batsmen "with the most terrifying bouncers I have ever seen," said Cardus. "The new ball might have been a red-hot explosive. But George Gunn walked out to this fearsome attack, and upper-cut a flier into the Ladies' Pavilion for six, over third man's head, standing on his tip-toes to do so. Whereat McDonald said: 'George, do that again and I'll knock your block off.' And George replied: 'Why, Ted, you couldn't knock the skin off a rice pudding.'"

But George Gunn was in no doubt that McDonald was the best of all fast bowlers that he faced.

After Gregory and McDonald faded, the pendulum swung back to England, who discovered Larwood and Voce and Tate to plague Australia; and the next really fast man to appear down under was McCormick. But between the wars three leg-spinners and an astonishingly versatile left-arm bowler served their country well: Arthur Mailey, Clarrie Grimmett, Bill O'Reilly and one of cricket's curiosities, L. O'B. "Chuck" Fleetwood-Smith, who turned to bowling left-arm "tweakers" when he broke his right arm.

Mailey and Grimmett were leg-spinners in the classic mould, although their methods and approach were so different as to make them appear miles apart. Mailey was slightly taller and used flight to a much greater degree, being almost uncanny in the way he could harness a breeze to his craft. In post-war years he never looked on length as essential to success, claiming that a ball spun viciously *must* do something different, and that even if it was a full toss or a long-hop, it would cause the batsman to fall into error.

Grimmett, with his short jerky approach, and action, would drop into a length at once, and maintain it to the end. Mailey brought his arm right over; Grimmett bowled almost roundarm. Mailey didn't care how many runs he gave away so long as he got the wickets in the end; Grimmett rarely bowled a loose ball and never on purpose. Mailey used flight to tempt batsmen down the pitch, but Grimmett would hardly ever do so, especially if he knew the man would attack. Against such a batsman he would push the ball through lower and quicker, and drive him back on his stumps. Grimmett took 39 wickets against England in Tests in Australia, and 67 in England. Mailey had 60 in Australia and 26 in England. But Grimmett's miserliness paid off in the end – he finished with 216 Test wickets in all in 37 Tests – figures surpassed only by Benaud, McKenzie and Lindwall, though each of these played in more than 60 Tests. Mailey's total was 99 from 21 Tests.

Big Bill O'Reilly and Sydney Barnes were assessed by Sir Donald

Bradman as the two greatest bowlers the world had ever known, and The Don, being an Australian, was inclined to give the benefit of the doubt to O'Reilly. There is no doubt he ranks in the first three Australians, all dubbed Australian-style with nicknames – "The Demon" Spofforth, "The Terror" Turner and "The Tiger" O'Reilly. Since the war, even in an age where metaphors abound and language is freer than it used to be, only one other bowler has earned himself a similar soubriquet – "Typhoon" Tyson, and he an Englishman. Even Thomson is just "Thommo".

O'Reilly's career coincided until the Second World War with Bradman's, and Sir Donald's admiration for him has always been unbounded. He first faced O'Reilly in 1926, on a concrete wicket at Bowral, in a Saturday afternoon fixture. "I survived his first few overs," writes The Don dryly, "more by luck than good management – and remained 234 not out at stumps. We continued the match the following Saturday at Wingello, and in the first over he bowled me round my legs

Don Bradman reckoned "Tiger" O'Reilly the greatest spinner of all.

before I had added to my score. I was amazed that a man could turn the ball with his grip."

That point was to baffle many a lesser batsman than Bradman. O'Reilly was well over six feet, delivered the ball with a swing of the arms which described a complete circle and when in action against the best batsmen gave the impression that he simply hated his opponents. If anything went wrong, he would grab the ball angrily, all his heart, soul, arms, legs and body would pour into the next ball as he spun the ball viciously, almost snarling at the poor batsman the while.

He did not grip the ball like the orthodox spinner, but like Barnes he held it more in the palm of the hand. His normal ball was a leg-break, which he could turn even on a mirror wicket. He bowled his googly and his top-spinner with exactly the same grip, the only clue being that with his "bosie" he would sometimes drop his right arm a little. As his right arm was revolving, his left was thrust forward, with the fingers spread out towards the batsman as though warning him to keep back. The googly could bounce like a tennis ball, often resulting in a simple catch to one of the two short legs he always had waiting. (Shades of Spoff once more.) He was so accurate that although he could some- times be hit, his close-up fielders were never in any real danger.

Fleetwood-Smith, who succeeded Clarrie Grimmett as O'Reilly's chief partner in the Australian attack, could also spin the ball remark- ably fiercely, making the ball twist and turn on the hardest of pitches. Often, though, he was inaccurate, and more than once Walter Ham- mond hit him clean out of the reckoning. But he took more than 500 wickets in first-class cricket, mainly for Victoria, and won at least two Test matches for Australia with his "chinamen" and "bosies".

It is not far from the truth to say that he was the last real spinner that Australia produced until Richie Benaud.

★   ★   ★   ★   ★

If the period before the First World War was the Golden Age of Engl- ish cricket, then between the wars, particularly insofar as batting was concerned, could well be known as The Age of Style. No, I have not forgotten Bradman in the Australian saga, as if anyone could. But I believe that he was unique, and stood on his own plateau far above other mortals of his era, and that he deserves a chapter all to himself.

Not that one should describe a batsman of the calibre of Sir Jack Hobbs or Walter Hammond as a lesser mortal. Both of them explored the very heights of batsmanship and added to them their own lustre: Hobbs with courage, the utmost skill and the grace born of balance and beautiful timing, and Hammond with fire and arrogance that matured into majestic dominance.

Jack Hobbs' career spanned the last days of W.G.'s and the early triumphs of Sir Donald Bradman. Hobbs made his first appearance for Surrey at The Oval against the Gentlemen, and by almost divine coincidence, the opposing skipper was W. G. Opening the batting with his mentor, Tom Hayward, he made 88, the top score in the match. He made 155 in his second match and 1300 in his first season. He shared in England's triumphs with the Foster/Barnes combination before the First World War, went through the testing by fire in the disastrous years just after it when Gregory and McDonald were on the rampage, and completed his international career in 1930. With various excellent partners, for whom later Hutton, for one, must have longed for, he set 166 century stands for the opening partnership, 66 times with Andrew Sandham, 40 with Hayward and with Sutcliffe 26. He made at least three hundreds against every county in the Championship, and twelve hundreds against Australia; and in all his long career (1905–34) he totalled 61,237 runs in 1315 innings for an average of 50.65, 197 hundreds – a record unlikely ever to be breached (Tom Graveney, the highest of post-war batsmen, mustered 47,793 and M. C. Cowdrey 42,719).

Hobbs' strength lay in his mastery of all the strokes, his amazingly quick eye and his ability (far more pronounced than Bradman's) to be able to reproduce his best form on all wickets. H. S. Altham wrote: "Of all batsmen, he was the most versatile; the glazed wickets of Sydney and Adelaide, the matting of Johannesburg and Durban, only enhanced his reputation."

Such was his consistency that in 1925, the year in which he passed W. G.'s record of 126 centuries, innings of 50 and upwards were greeted with newspaper placards announcing "HOBBS FAILS AGAIN".

E. W. Swanton has explained how Hobbs was the bridge between the old batting style and the new. He was brought up in the classical tradition of W. G. and Fry, and Ranji, when the backlift was high, and the off-side strokes were the jewels in the batsman's crown. Then, as he was still climbing to the top, came the revolution in technique needed to cope not only with the leg-spin and dipping googlies of Bosanquet and his wrist-spinning disciples, but also the advent of the speed merchants and the swing bowlers, exploring and developing the earlier art of George Hirst.

Neville Cardus said, in a radio broadcast given on Sir Jack's 70th Birthday, "he was the first batsman really to master the new bowling. Hobbs combined the classic freedom of forward play and full swing of the bat with the necessary adaptation to defeat the googly and late swerve; that is to say, he also demonstrated the use of the delayed

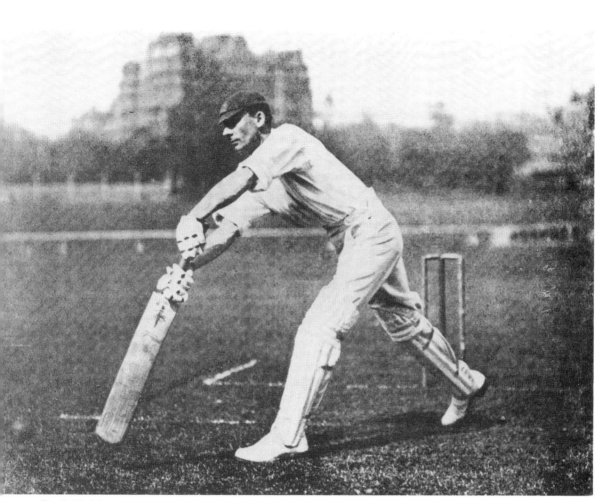

Jack Hobbs, who dominated English batting throughout the 'twenties. His natural grace was evident in every shot and, like Bradman, he had the gift of early sight.

defensive stroke, legs and pads over the wicket, with handle of the bat held loosely, so that if the ball got through the spin would be killed and rendered as null and void as if it had collided with a sandbag."

Hobbs could hit as hard through the covers as anyone, and pull with a vehemence only excelled by Bradman, from a rather open but still relaxed stance. This is Swanton's tribute, and it will serve: "In the last resort the difference between talent and mastery is a matter of character. Hobbs brought to cricket an ascetic self-discipline which in tight corners expressed itself perfectly in his play. He was a man of conspicuous personal modesty; but his pride in his position as, in every sense, England's number one, gave his batting an aura of serenity communicable to his opponents and to his fellows. None ever saw

67

Hobbs rattled, or in a hurry. And if he was anxious, it never showed.

"There was a quiet dignity about him which had its roots in mutual respect; for others as for himself. He had the natural good manners of a Christian and a sportsman, and the esteem in which, in his day, his profession came to be held owed much to the man who for the best part of a quarter of a century was its undisputed leader."

One cannot mention Hobbs, of course, without saying, in the same breath, Sutcliffe. His career coincided exactly with the inter-war period. Sutcliffe made a century on his first visit to Lord's, for Yorkshire on an atrocious pitch; he made another three years later for England v the Rest (the first time he batted with Hobbs) and 122 in the opening stand, with Hobbs, of 268 in his first Test match, against South Africa. He was vigilant, concentrated, and businesslike, but never slow. Three times in a season he accumulated – that is the only word – more than 3000 runs. Runs flowed from his bat in a ceaseless torrent. He lacked the polished artistry of Hobbs or the princely quality of Hammond, and in true Yorkshire tradition, he loved a fight.

More than any Englishman since Grace, Walter Hammond approached the majesty and all-embracing talents of W. G. Grace. In an age of shirt-front wickets and great batsmanship he was the one who would fill a cricket-ground anywhere in the world and send the crowds away refreshed and satisfied – not to say sated – by the power and the glory of his batting. People used to say of Bradman that while he was batting, his perfection was so inevitable, that he would send spectators away for a beer out of sheer boredom. Sometimes, in his later years, with the cares of England on his shoulders and ill-health his companion, Hammond could do that too, as he stayed in for hour after hour, treating every ball with the utmost courtesy and consideration; but in his salad days, and in his prime too, no-one ever left his seat in case he should miss one of those majestic cover-drives off front *or* back foot. Even in the trials of his autumn, he was incapable of an ugly stroke. Nothing he did was laboured and his concentration never cramped his poise. Tom Graveney, when he was at his greatest (which was very good indeed), was just common-or-garden Hammond, who once told Cardus after making a large score on a perfect wicket: "It was too easy."

Cardus recalls: "He emerged into maturity just as Test matches were changing in temper and attitude according to what I shall herewith call the Jardinian theory, the theory taught by the strongest-willed of all the England captains, the theory of the survival not so much of the fittest but of the most durable. The great batsman for the purpose of Test matches, according to the theory, was he who stayed in for hours and compiled large quantities of runs, not necessarily by command and beautiful strokes but by the processes of attrition.*

"Hammond remained to the end a batsman handsome to look at, a pedigree batsman, monumental and classic. But I shall continue to try to remember well the young Hammond who in 1927, when the Gloucestershire cause seemed lost beyond repair, hooked the pace of McDonald with a savage power I had seldom seen before and have never seen since."

Gloucestershire, with 2 wickets down in their second innings, were only 44 ahead, and Lancashire looked certain winners.

"From the first over of the day, bowled by McDonald with the velocity and concentration of a man determined to get back to Castle Irwell in time to back a certain winner at five to one against. Hammond drove five fours from five consecutive balls. The sixth ball would also have counted for four, but it was fielded on the boundary's edge at the sightscreen behind McDonald's arm. A straight-drive from the first over off the most dangerous fast bowler of many decades! Hammond punished McDonald so contumaciously that short bumpers were soon whizzing about Hammond's head. He hooked them time after time as ferociously as they were discharged at him. I watched this death-or-glory innings standing in the dusty earth near the Manchester end of the ground, near long leg. Several of Hammond's hooks crashed to earth, sending gravel flying about us like shrapnel. In some three hours Hammond scored 187, with no chance, four sixes and 24 fours."

Eleven years later, Hammond hit another very fast bowler, McCormick, and the left-handed "tweaker" Fleetwood-Smith for 240, his greatest Test innings, and the whole ground stood to him. And in 1928–29, on his first Australian tour, under A. P. F. Chapman, he hit a world record Test series aggregate of 905, for an average of 113.2. His Test innings were 44 and 28; 251; 200 and 32 (run out); 119 not out and 177; 38 and 16. His career total was 50,493, for an average of 56.10. And he was a fine fast-medium bowler too, and the finest slip field of his or any other generation.

"It is the sign of the master that (a) his movements of foot and hand are instinctive and often unnoticeable and (b) that he seems, whether batting to the fastest bowling or fielding to the swiftest and most awkward catches, to have all the time in the world. When Hammond caught ten Surrey batsmen in one match in 1928 and eight Worcestershire batsmen four years later, he and the bowler (Charlie Parker) between them had exerted a kind of mesmerism which was nearly irresistible and the catcher did not move till the last tiniest fraction of a second."

*How Jardine would have admired Geoffrey Boycott!

"The faster they come, the harder he hit them" – Frank Woolley's hook, to perfection.

So wrote A. A. Thomson, who in *Cricketers of My Times* added: "In the days of the Gentlemen v Players matches he was one of the few who at one time or another played on each side. That he was a gentleman in the deepest sense was unquestionable; equally unquestionable was his status as a superb player; and, on whichever side he played, he was an aristocrat."

★   ★   ★   ★   ★

Three left-handers stood out above all others during the 'twenties and 'thirties, all of differing characters and approach to the game. The most dashing of them all, a man with the very grace of the willow tree at his command, was Frank Woolley, the evergreen Kent batsman who charmed the very cover off the ball as he "whispered instructions to it" on the way to the boundary. Robertson-Glasgow said you had to ration the superlatives when you were writing about Woolley's batting, for otherwise you would probably have used them up before you'd got past the second over. He felt that Woolley probably preferred them fast and short; then they went that much more quickly to the boundary.

He was very tall, and turned what to an ordinary batsman would be a good-length ball into a half-volley. Like Tony Greig of today, his height, and great reach, made a nonsense of length. His defence, when he wanted it to be, was immaculate, and he could hit almost with the power of Hammond off the back foot; but his left-handed fluency was unrivalled until Neil Harvey appeared on the scene for Australia in the late 'forties, and Sobers burst on the West Indian scene a few years later; and his late-cut was later, and more graceful, than anyone's, certainly within living memory. Even bowlers liked bowling to him, though the Lord knows why, for although he was thought likely always to "give the bowler a chance" by going for his shots from the first ball, apart from Hobbs, no-one has ever made more runs on the cricket field (58,969) – including the thousand 28 times, the same as W. G. And as a bowler, he once took 10 wickets in a Test match for 49 runs – 5 in each innings.

Second in my list of great left-handers was C. P. ("Philip") Mead, of Hampshire, less attractive to watch than Woolley, but one of the most consistent batsmen of all time. He played from 1905 to 1936 and, surprisingly, in only seventeen Tests in all that time. No-one has made more runs for an English county (48,892 at an averate 48.84) – higher than Woolley's. He was rarely spectacular, but his batting had an air of inevitability, with the essential mark of class in that he always seemed to have time to make the stroke. Unlike Hobbs, however, who had two strokes for every ball, Mead had just one – and it was always the right one. All the bowlers of his time said his bat always seemed extra wide, and he had the ability to judge to a fraction of an inch whether a swinging ball would (or would not) hit the stumps. In this, possibly the man with similar ability is the Australian Greg Chappell. Like Chappell, Mead had the ability to angle his bat away from the ball at the very last moment to allow it to swing past the stumps.

And last, but by no means least, there was Maurice Leyland, broad of beam, Yorkshire by birth, tradition, brogue and humour, who was brought back so many times to stiffen an England middle order that (just as it does today in the 'seventies) so often sagged like a rag doll with the stuffing taken out. Leyland, like Sutcliffe, was a fighter, and he could stonewall all day with the best, but he was capable, when the need was there, of brilliant hitting, particularly on the off side. He was a fine exponent of the cover-drive, taking the ball "on the up", his feet moving into position in a flash, his body virtually motionless as he played the stroke with rhythmic timing. And he had the left-hander's pull to perfection.

He was also a vastly down-to-earth character, credited with the undying remark, in conversation with other famous players, about fast bowling: "Fact is, none of us likes fast bowlin' – but some of us doesn't let on."

No doubt others, older than I, who can bring to the years between the wars more mature memories than those of a young schoolboy, will point to the omissions in this list. Where, for example, is Patsy Hendren, the Middlesex imp of mischief; Eddie Paynter, pint-sized but after Hammond the greatest hooker of fast bowling of his day; the Coxes of Sussex, or Hugh Bartlett too? Where is Wellard, who hit 500 sixes in his career for Somerset? Where are the incomparable Hutton, the mercurial Compton and his "twin", Edrich? The last three we shall come to later, as their careers overlapped the Second World War. But for the rest, for me, the style-setting Englishmen of an era as rich in talent in its own way as the Golden Age, were Hobbs, and after him, Hammond and Woolley.

★   ★   ★   ★   ★

England's bowlers of the same period, it must be admitted, had to cope with Macartney, McCabe and Bradman at the height of their very considerable powers, and perhaps it is not surprising that only intermittently did they conquer in their battles with the oldest foe. When they did, it was when Harold Larwood was at his peak, and again when the genius of Hedley Verity was in its full flower. With these two go a number of others: Maurice Tate, Bill Voce, Bill Bowes and Alf Gover of those who bowled fast, and (briefly) Kenneth Farnes, Charles Parker and Tom Goddard of Gloucestershire and A. P. Freeman of Kent, all three of whom failed to gain proper recognition at international level.

72

But they were all masters of their various crafts.

Throughout the 'thirties, the batsman was master, as Hobbs, Hammond, Sutcliffe and the rest kept piling up their 3000 runs a season, but Verity and Bowes regularly got between 150 and 200 wickets apiece, and Parker and Goddard, spinning away with wily expertise, took 200 wickets each nine times. Freeman took over 200 wickets *every year* from 1928 to 1935. With Freeman bowling and Ames keeping wicket for Kent, even on perfect pitches, the combination was unfair, most batsmen felt, almost magic. In one match in 1934 (a golden summer similar to that of 1976) Kent scored 592 for 6 against Gloucestershire against both Goddard (who took 183 wickets in the season) and Parker (well over 100), and Ames hit 295; Freeman's figures were 5 for 18 and 6 for 32. In this batsman's year there were four hat-tricks, Verity twice took 9 wickets in an innings and once, against Essex at Leyton, 17 wickets in a day.

But enough of figures. Harold Larwood, like Freddie Trueman after him, came up from the pits when he was eighteen to become a Nottinghamshire fast bowler in partnership with Bill Voce. Three years later he played his first Test match, in 1926. He was short for a fast bowler – well under six feet – but he had a long reach, and his smooth, rhythmic action hurled the ball down at a thunderous pace. His secret was in his pace, but also in his control of length and direction. Few quick bowlers (of much slower pace) ever had the control of Larwood (Lindwall had it and Lillee developed it) and possibly only he had the intelligence *and* control to bowl to the Jardine bodyline plan and bring it off consistently. (Jardine added to the menacing bowling seven or eight fielders in a double ring on the leg side.) Larwood's best haul in a Test innings was 6 for 32 at Brisbane in 1928, five years before the bodyline series, but the dull-paced pitches of the time and the modern long-term batting skills developed by Bradman and Ponsford and reduced him near to being dropped. However, he was part of the Jardine plan to win the Ashes in 1933, and in that most dramatic of all series he took 33 wickets at a cost of 19 apiece – at that time a record for a fast bowler.

He was able to exploit the bodyline theory more intelligently and more dangerously than anyone else. Getting batsmen to cock up catches off balls rearing off short of a length (and aimed *at their bodies*) was not the chief purpose of his strategy. He used bumpers scientifically to soften up their defences, to divide their attention between playing the ball and saving their skins. Once he got them ducking and weaving they were easier prey for the sudden, well-pitched-up straight ball, especially if he could get them to back away from the stumps. Sixteen of his 33 wickets in that series were bowled, and two l.b.w.

Ray Robinson wrote that the pundit's advice to the batsman that

Harold Larwood – few fast bowlers have ever had his control. Lindwall and Lillee were his successors in style; and Tyson, also successful at cowing Australian batsmen.

what was needed to play Larwood was a stout heart and a straight bat was soon disproved; there was an even greater call for a cross bat and a tough hide.

Larwood won that series for Jardine but it cost him dear. He broke down on the fourth day of the last Test, having bowled his heart out and batted for two and a half hours for 98 in England's innings as well. He was never the same bowler again, and eventually retired aged only 33. And Jardine, his iron-willed captain, went back to England and after one season, out of favour and out of Test cricket. Bodyline was killed by official ukase and did not raise its head again, although in recent years its ghost has risen for both West Indies and Australia.

Stan McCabe, who hit 187 against Larwood at his fastest (as we have seen), said himself that he'd got away with it once, but couldn't again, and in fact in his other nine innings against bodyline he made a total of 198.

Keith Miller and R. S. Whitington, analysing bodyline, said that Larwood's version of it was never mastered on the pitch. They reckoned there were five alternative methods to be adopted to cope with it:

1. To dodge, or duck heads and shoulders away from the paths of the bumpers, keeping the bat out of the way too.
2. To stand up and take the bruising balls on their bodies.
3. To play defensively at the shoulder and head-high fliers with their bats held perpendicularly in front of their faces and upper chest.
4. To hook the bowler out of the attack.
5. To step back some feet to the leg and slash cross-batted at the ball to force it away into the unguarded field on the off side.

If batsmen adopted (1) and (2) they never scored any runs and with (2) particularly, they would certainly be hurt, if not maimed or even killed.

Method (3) led immediately to a catch to one of the four or five short fielders.

Method (4), the one Macartney used, could be occasionally successful, but was also doubly risky unless you had a very quick eye and bat; in any case there was the outer ring of leg-side fielders waiting for a catch.

Method (5), used by Bradman in that same series with considerable success (he scored 396 in four bodyline Tests at an average of over 50), was also risky, as you left your stumps wide open for the occasional straight ball or yorker.

The climax of the bodyline tour occurred at Adelaide, and it was the incident which led to trans-oceanic cables, the near calling-off of the tour and, mercifully, to the eventual outlawing of bodyline itself. Lar-

Which is which? Left: Australian Ted McDonald, in 1921. Right: Alec Bedser, who alone maintained England's bowling dignity in the years after the Second World War. Note the immaculate STYLE in both cases.

wood, bowling to Woodfull, the Australian captain, with a normal fast bowler's field, felled the batsman with a short ball that hit him under the heart. Painfully, Woodfull got to his feet and took guard again. As Larwood began his run-up, Jardine stopped him, motioned the fielders to the leg trap set for bodyline, and ordered Larwood to bowl his bumpers. In later, less disciplined years and countries, such an action would have lead to a full-scale riot.

Even the staid Adelaide crowd erupted. Had one person jumped the fence, the England team would have been mobbed. But good sense prevailed, and although relations between the two countries were strained for a while, peace and good fellowship were fully restored by the next tour, under G. O. Allen. Not only was there no bodyline, but England *lost*.

After Barnes and before Bedser, the greatest seam bowler of his age was Maurice Tate, of Sussex and England, the biggest-hearted, unluckiest bowler whom Sussex ever sacked. To this day, when the sea-fret creeps around the ground at Hove, there are still whispers among the old, old men sitting quietly on the seats under the old, old pavilion, that Maurice Tate's ghost is walking again as John Snow takes the wickets "young Chub" used to.

Three times Tate took over 200 wickets and scored 1000 runs in a season. He did the ordinary "double" eight times. He played in 39 Tests. He scored 23 centuries in his 21,584 runs and in five countries he bowled more than 25,000 overs and took 2784 wickets at an average of 18.15 in the days of plumb wickets and great batsmen.

He was a big man, a great man in cricket. He cut the ball both ways off a length, and he beat the bat more times than any other bowler living. He often beat the wicket too, "by a coat of varnish", and to a batsman the ball seemed, more often than not, to leave the pitch faster than it had left the hand. Twenty years later Alec Bedser was likened to Tate more than to any other bowler.

When he entered first-class cricket, Bill Voce, Nottingham and England, was a slow left-arm spinner. But when he toured Australia with Jardine's team, he was (contrary to most progessions) fast enough to play chopping-block to the Larwood axe. His part in that miserable tour was to bowl as fast as he could; length did not matter provided he kept the ball on the leg stump – or even outside it. He took 15 wickets at 27 runs apiece, bowling to order, and went back from that tour with the unfortunate reputation of being nothing more than a slinger.

But Voce was a much better bowler than that, and by the time the tour of 1936–37 came around, he needed no bodyline tactics to help him. On the first tour he bowled round the wicket; now he went over, and he took 6 wickets for only 41, his main killer being not the bumper, but the ball which moved off the pitch towards the slips. In the second innnings, he and G. O. Allen sent the Australians back for 58 – and Voce's figures were 4 for 16.

Hedley Verity was, after Wilfred Rhodes, the very best left-arm bowler England ever produced. In his short career, ended by death in the Second World War, he took 1956 wickets at 14.87 runs apiece, including 144 wickets in 40 Tests. In Australia in 1932–33 he was seldom needed when bodyline was all the rage, but when Larwood broke down in the final Test Verity took 5 wickets for 33 in 19 overs, turning a score of 115 for one to 182 all out. In county games he twice took all 10 wickets in an innings, once for only 10 runs. Nottingham-shire were the victims.

He was tall and lean, using all his inches to achieve a high delivery with perfect control of line, length and pace. He was slow-medium rather than genuinely slow, but he could drop his pace when the conditions suited it. He was a student of cricket, and owed his success to persistent thought which sharpened his natural ability. Don Bradman said that Verity had no breaking point. He never wilted under punishment, but schemed away, planning the batsman's downfall. On true, hard wickets he sometimes looked somewhat negative; but he was not. Miracles took a little longer, that was all.

The great Hedley Verity. His modern "descendant" is Derek Underwood.

4

The Don

I did not see Don Bradman bat until his last season, 1948. But my childhood was filled with the wonder of his batsmanship, in newspapers, in the old newsreels, on the radio which we called wireless. It was three months after I had left the army, having seen no first-class cricket since I was twelve, before the war, and I was about to begin my own, undistinguished efforts as a club batsman and wicketkeeper for Chelmsford. I had also been a journalist for two months. So when an old friend, Peter Smith, the Essex and England leg-spinner, offered me a lift to Southend to watch the first day of the Essex match against the Australians, I jumped at the chance.

The Australians won the toss and batted on a shirt-front wicket that gleamed as I sat on the boundary at square leg, basking under a sun which shone out of a cloudless sky. The Australians made 721 that day, the highest score ever in a single day's cricket, and Bradman, the master, made 187 of them. He used every stroke in the book, and several of his own invention; and he did not give a chance. Another leg-spinner, Frank Vigar, who could turn the ball a foot on a sheet of glass, but who suffered a little when it came to accuracy, was given an over before lunch. Bradman watched his first ball go by. Then he hit the next five, in succession, to the square-leg boundary. It mattered not where the ball pitched, what it was designed to do, or not to do, each one whistled to one side or other of me. But the end of the over, four fielders were patrolling the area between long-on and long leg. None of them could move to stop the ball as it streaked across the grass. It wasn't cricket, it was murder. At some time soon after lunch, with the score at 245 for 2, Keith Miller strolled out to the wicket, Bill Brown the opening batsman having just tired of the sport and surrendered his wicket to Trevor Bailey.

Miller strolled out to the wicket, his bat over his shoulder, tapped his bat once in the crease as a gesture to the umpire in place of taking guard, and stood with his bat over his shoulder watching Bailey run to the wicket. The ball was of good length, and straight. Miller watched

Don Bradman's typical pull to leg. It's not just the stroke itself here which denotes the style of the man – look at the balance, the balletic feet, the forward movement of the body and the concentration of the eyes.

the ball hit the wicket, his bat still over his shoulder, and strolled back to the pavilion. Someone asked him why – "I don't like taking candy from kids", said Miller, and went off to the races.

Bradman, in his whole career, could never have done that. He could never have said, as Hammond did: "It's too easy." His cricket, from first to last, was total dedication. Matches were meant to be won, and won, and won by the largest margin possible. In 1948 his objective was to lead the first Australian side through an entire English tour, unbeaten. It was also his objective to go out, in this his retirement year, with the trumpets blazing. He scored more runs than any other Australian on the tour (2428) and after it was all over, there could be only one regret. Eric Hollies bowled him for a duck in his last Test innings, which meant that his career Test average, instead of being

80

exactly 100, ended at only (!) **99.94**. And he walked from that blob cheered all the way to the pavilion, with as little evident emotion and as much quiet dignity as he had shown in any of his 80 Test innings.

He had a reputation for ruthlessness, but that wasn't really deserved. His attitude was simply perfectionist. Pity didn't come into it; it was illogical to Bradman not to win any match by the largest lawful margin. He asked no more of his team than he was prepared to give himself, but that is not to say that he didn't ask more of some of them than they might have had it in them to give.

"The most ruthless element in his composition was his own self-discipline," wrote A. A. Thomson. "When the bat was in his hand, the prodigious, but economical power which he put into every stroke had no more connection with mere slogging than had Jessop's scientific hitting. Bradman's method of propulsion had the precision of a modern machine-gun. In its context, his batting was the modern machine-gun. It was the perfect co-ordination of hand and eye and foot with the quickest reflexes ever possessed by any cricketer.

"His cricketing life was dedicated to the elementary (and elemental) proposition that every ball sent down was destined for punishment. He did not, of course, hit every ball he received to the boundary, but he hit infinitely more fours and sixes than the ordinary batsman who waits for 'the right ball to hit'. The difference naturally depended on the batsman's definition of the word 'right'. For Bradman most deliveries were the right deliveries."

Jack Fingleton, who played many a long innings with Bradman as Australia's opening batsman in the 'thirties, says that the Don's one weakness was some inability to bat on a sticky wicket. But in 1932 he scored a lovely 71 on a bad Sydney pitch. Fingleton reckons that Bradman's psychology changed if the pitch was affected by rain. It was the only thing that could disturb a cool, calculating analytical mind in its immaculate judgment; although Fingleton also reckoned that Bradman was equally affected by the bodyline saga. He wrote: "That historic happening in cricket was unimpeachably because of Bradman's influence and dominance in cricket. Bodyline was specially prepared, nurtured for and expended on him, and in consequence, his technique underwent a change quicker than might have been the case with the passage of time. Bodyline plucked something vibrant from his art." But Fingleton went on to point out that soon after the bodyline year, Bradman became the Australian captain, and often Bradman the batsman had to become subservient to Bradman the captain. "In all periods of his area, though his technique changed considerably, Bradman's remained to the last the most remarkable appetite for runs the game has ever known."

5
After Bradman

Learie Constantine was one of the very few cricketers in history – Garfield Sobers was another – who by his batting, bowling or fielding could change the whole state of the game from incipient defeat to victory. His talents shone with increasing brilliance from 1919's small beginnings in Trinidad to 1939 at The Oval in the last Test played before the last war. In the meantime he had electrified the Lancashire League, outside the County Championship the toughest club cricket competition in Britain; and afterwards he became in succession barrister, his country's ambassador to the Court of St James, and (deservedly if anyone ever did) Lord Constantine.

First, he was a fieldsman. Under the eye of H. G. B. Austin, the "father" of West Indian cricket, and with the help and encouragement of Jack Hobbs and Pelham Warner, he made himself into the finest cover point the world had ever seen – even to those who could remember Trumper. At first he was little more than a slogger, with an occasional inspirational shot he devised for himself on the spur of the moment, and blossomed into an attacking batsman reminiscent indeed of Trumper and Macartney and Jessop. And finally, he became, for several overs at least and well into his thirties, the fastest bowler in the world after Larwood. He was even capable of launching, in 1934, with Martindale, a bodyline attack that broke R. E. S. Wyatt's jaw, laid Hammond's chin open and moved no less than Jack Hobbs to comment that he was glad that England had been given some of their own medicine.

Constantine in the field was so fast that he made difficult chances look easy – and held chances no other fielder would have thought of approaching. Colin Bland, the big Rhodesian, equalled him for speed and surpassed him with accuracy of throw; Clive Lloyd was his peer but never his superior, for about five years until illness slowed him (I once saw him run, dive, stop a certain four, and throw a batsman out, from a sitting position on the grass, fullpitch on to the middle stump, from 45 yards, flat as an arrow). Of them all, it was said that they were worth their place in any side for their fielding alone and (a moment of personal pride) the same has been said of my son Paul (Cambridge University and Sussex). But as Constantine made thousands of runs and took hundreds of wickets, the theory didn't have to be tested.

Constantine brought to the game a terrific dynamism and a hatful of unorthodox strokes. He had the eye, hand and reflexes that were outside the reach of the ordinary human frame. He made hooks and pulls from every conceivable (and some inconceivable) position and on occasions would even overhead-smash the ball to the boundary as if he'd been wielding a tennis racket instead of an unyielding piece of willow.

He bowled without bothering to remove his cap. He didn't roll up his sleeves, but kept them buttoned at the wrists. He seemed to consist of a pair of long legs surmounted by broad shoulders, with long arms dangling from each corner, and he bowled furiously fast with a flowing action propelled from a bounding run packed with energy.

A. A. Thomson recalls his last Test at The Oval: "Picture Arthur Wood, of Yorkshire, keeping wicket for England, crouching behind, itching for the stumping chance that never came. At the wicket Constantine had made 79 in an indecently short time and by strokes that were all against the laws of physics and was rampaging to score far more in much less. Going down in his own individual way he made contact with a shortish ball from perks in a gigantic hook stroke which soared in the general direction of long leg. As the ball rose virtually into outer space, Arthur turned and ran, pads, gloves and all. By the time the ball started coming down, the batsman had run two, and Arthur was standing in front of the pavilion railings. As it finally descended, he took a neat catch.

"'By god,' he murmured in a sigh of relief. 'It's lucky I was standing back.'"

The second West Indian to claim world renown in the 'thirties was known, with some reason, as "the black Bradman" – George Headley. In his first three games against an MCC touring team captained by L. H. (later Lord) Tennyson, he hit 71, 211 and 71 again. When the MCC sent a strong side in 1929–30, in the first representative game he scored 176 and in the third, he hit two centuries. In the fourth, when West Indies were set 836 to win the game, he scored 223 and saved the game. His aggregate for the series was 703, average 87.87. The following year he toured Australia and made two hundreds; then he was back home to play in another series against another Tennyson team. In four innings he *averaged* 361.50 – with 344 not out, 84, 155 not out and 140. In 1933 he toured England for the first time and scored seven tour centuries.

He was likened to Bradman not only because of his immense appe-

On the drive
above: Walter Hammond – Imperious.
below: Charlie Macartney – Devastating.

above: Learie Constantine – Grandiloquent.
below: Barrie Richards – Impossible.
(NB. All four batsmen were geniuses)

tite for runs; he was neat and trim, short and quick. He could command off the back foot nearly all the strokes that the classic batsman makes off the front foot. He could hook, cut, drive a ball to the ropes by the power of his wrists alone and without opening his shoulders. Sometimes when making a cut or a cover-drive his bat seemed to be right over the stumps and both his feet off the ground at once. And he had one major advantage over Bradman – he positively liked bad wickets.

He has said, and all who saw him play can testify to the truth of it, that he did not care who bowled at him; right, left, slow, fast, they all came alike.

"On a bad wicket it is you and the bowler. If he pitched up you had to drive; if he pitched short you had to turn and hook. No nonsense."

C. L. R. James wrote that Headley told him that the night before a Test innings he rarely slept more than an hour or two. "But he isn't suffering from insomnia, not in the least. This fantastic man is busy playing his innings the next day. The fast bowler will swing from leg. He plays a stroke. Then the bowler will come in from the off. He plays the stroke to correspond. The bowler will shorten. George hooks or cuts. Verity will keep a length on or just outside the off stump. George will force him away getting back to cut, and must be on guard not to go too greedily at a loose ball – that is how in Tests he most fears he will lose his innings. Langridge will flight the ball. Down the pitch for the drive. So he goes through every conceivable ball and makes a stroke to correspond. This cricket strategist works on the Napoleonic principle that if a general is taken by surprise by anything that happens on a battlefield, then he is a bad general."

*   *   *   *   *

Cricket was played on the Indian sub-continent as early as the eighteenth century, but, in spite of the examples given to it by the successes of Ranjitsinhji and his nephew Duleepsinhji, it was not until 1911 that a representative side under the Maharajah of Patiala, a keen sportsman himself, toured England. The criticism made by Indians of both Duleep and Ranji was that they did not do anything overtly to encourage the Indian game itself; and it was not until Jack Hobbs and Herbert Sutcliffe made a special tour of the country in 1931–32 that enthusiasm was kindled which led to the first Tests being played between the two countries.

The same could not be said of the Nawabs of Pataudi; the father played for both England and India, and his son captained India after

86

the Second World War. Before it, however, several Indian cricketers made their mark on the world scene; among them a remarkable young batsman, Mushtaq Ali.

Mushtaq was one of a fine young band of cricketers who opened India's international cricket book, among the others being the batsman Amarnath and Merchant, bowlers Amar Singh and Mahomed Nissar (who was probably the fastest they have yet produced). Mushtaq Ali was tall, impetuous and a great improvisor of strokes. It was nothing to see him hit a good-length ball for six over the bowler's head, and then pat a couple of half-volleys down the pitch defensively. But on his day he had an uncommonly good eye and could murder the best of bowling.

Lala Amarnath had a chequered career which included being sent home from a tour in disgrace, but he became captain of India after the war. He was an all-rounder – a right-hand batsman with an elegant style. He was the first batsman to score a century in a Test for India and in 1937–38 he hit three successive hundreds against Lord Tennyson's team. Vijay Merchant was another fine batsman who spanned the war. He opened the innings with Mushtaq, and there could not have been a more contrasting pair. Mushtaq, tall, elegant, impetuous, and Merchant, much shorter, quiet, contemplative, but a batsman with all the strokes. The pair had four attributes in common – strong strokes to leg, artistry in cutting, quick sighting of the ball and nimble footwork. Together they put on 203 – of which Ali made 112 in 150 minutes against England in the second innings of the Manchester Test in 1936, a record for an opening partnership against England playing at home.

But the outstanding cricketer of all was C. K. Nayudu, for many years the virtual dictator of Indian cricket, and always a subject and initiator of controversy, which has always dogged India's progress. Nayudu, or "C. K." as he was known to four decades of Indian cricket, was a true original. In the 'twenties the older school of Indian batsmanship was orthodox, after the English style. But Nayudu had his own ideas about batting. It was not only a matter of textbook stances, elbow up, left leg forward, and so on, but of using the whole body, wrists and feet especially, in order to improvise strokes. The bowler placed his field to contain the batsman's strokes, and Nayudu's object was to beat it, to hit the offside ball to leg, to loft the ball over the fielders's heads if he couldn't beat them along the ground. "India," he wrote once, "can ill afford to neglect this style of batting since her oriental genius is noted for its venturesomeness and greater repertoire of shots than are mentioned in the textbooks. Indians can never regard themselves as cricketers if they are not brilliant."

And he proved so himself.

And there was one other character, Ramji of Rajkot in Kathiawar, a fast bowler so fast that Arthur Gilligan, skipper of the 1926 MCC touring team, was believed to have asked his opposing captai n to take him off while his batsmen were still alive and uninjured. One story had it that he once bowled a bumper at the Maharajah of Patiala, having failed to get his wicket by repeatedly hitting him on the pads, and laid the Maharajah out. He then departed the state in a great hurry and was never invited there again.

And then came Hutton and Compton. Both Leonard Hutton and Denis Compton were established as brilliant batsman of the younger generation well before the Second World War. They, unlike Farnes and Verity, survived that particular holocaust to become the foundations upon which English cricket was rebuilt.

Of the two, Hutton was the pure stylist, the batsman who carried the textbook of every stroke to its ultimate perfection; unhurried, graceful, at times adding to his immaculacy a patina of glory. In 1938, in that interminable Test at The Oval, when Bradman broke his ankle trying to bowl on an everlasting wicket seemingly made of marble, he made 364 runs, the world's record score in a Test match until Garfield Sobers surpassed him by one run for West Indies against Pakistan at Kingston twenty years later.

One measure of his greatness was that he batted more than half his career with a shortened left forearm, having to revise his whole style to accommodate the injury. More than that, he played in England sides that were usually woefully short of "class". His peak season, apart from his marvellous innings at The Oval in 1938, was 1949, when he scored 3429 runs, twice exceeding 1000 runs in one month, and in his whole career he scored over 40,000 runs, nearly 7000 in Tests.

In his later years, particularly when he became captain of England, Hutton's critics were accustomed to accuse him of having developed a defensive mentality. Rather, like Jardine, he developed a strategy to win back the Ashes in 1953 (the first time since 1933 – it was a long enough gap) and to hold them in the famous "Tyson tour" of Australia in the following winter. His devised tactic using his fast bowlers, even on wickets apparently ideally suited to the spinners, paid off; but it led to a ritual dropping of the over rate and the slowing-down of much Test cricket, with subsequent and consequent effects on county cricket in England. Slow play coupled with a lack of success in the field nearly took English cricket into oblivion as the crowds fell away and the interest died in the late 'fifties and early 'sixties.

The second great batsman of the period was Denis Compton, who, like Jessop and Trumper and Macartney and Headley before him, made his own rules with a cricket bat and then broke them with astonishing insouciance. If Hutton was the Beethoven of his day, Compton was

Chopin, all light and air and exquisite grace. No-one who saw him turn a full-blooded drive at the last split second into a late-cut past first slip's *left* hand, or turn a full-toss outside the off stump into the finest of leg-glances could deny his genius. And yet he was capable of grim defence, as his two greatest Test match centuries against Australia in 1948's lost cause proved beyond doubt.

E. W. Swanton wrote of Hutton and Compton: "They were as different in type as in temperament, the one often puritanically correct, yet in his more expansive moments putting a rich bloom on the orthodox, and occasionally releasing all his inhibitions in a rich cascade of strokes. If Len Hutton was the pride of the North, Compton epitomised the Cockney wit and gaiety of the London Crowd; defiance, daring, improvisation, charm."

No post-war cricketer could have given more pleasure, and yet he had (in common with Geoffrey Boycott) one weakness. Trevor Bailey, a "character" of those years in England's team in quite a different mould, but an exceptional judge of cricket and cricketers with an unexpected sense of humour, described it in an article in *Playfair Cricket Monthly*. It was in "Compton's year", when he made more runs and scored more centuries (eighteen) than anyone in the history of the game:

"At the close of that summer when it was 'roses, roses all the way' I found myself batting with Denis against the South Africans in the Hastings Festival. Thousands turned up mainly in the hope of seeing him break the record. My one fear was that I should run him out, which seemed to be the only thing likely to prevent him achieving this feat.

"I was also aware that an event of this nature was by no means improbable as the golden boy's calling was unpredictable in the extreme and it had been remarked, with every justification, that his first call merely meant that he was prepared to open negotiations. Fortunately we managed to avoid this calamity largely through some unexpected co-operation from the South African fieldsmen.

"It was less satisfactory some years later in a Test match at Old Trafford, when Denis had me halfway down the wicket after his first alternative, halted me there with a frantic 'wait', and had me slightly puzzled as he passed me at full speed saying 'no!' On my way back to the pavilion I realised that I had become yet another victim of the Compton three-call trick."

Bailey himself, of course, if not the original "Barnacle", was a batsman of exceptional durability and stubbornness, in strict line from Scotton, and a lively, intelligent, and stylish fast-medium bowler. Between 1949 and 1959, he was the veritable sheet-anchor of the England side, his marathon innings if never examples of attractive batting

The Off-drive through the years

above: Golden Age power and timing from Arthur Shrewsbury, the top "pro" of his day.

below: The sheer beauty of Len Hutton's off drive made men forget love-affairs and wars alike.

left: Ted Dexter scorched the grass with his driving.

right: Rare aggression from Bill Lawry – sunniest character and dourest batsman Australia has produced since Bannerman. He scored so many runs they called him the "accumulator".

91

nevertheless the very acme of defiance and the model of the forward defensive prod. Yet it is on record that he once scored 200 runs in a day for Essex at Colchester – on a wet wicket!

The Cockney sparrow – Denis Compton pulls a four to leg.

"Tall, good-looking and confident in everything he did" – Peter May was the stylist of his day.

But after Hutton the three most potent, influential and, from the point of view of style, the most effective batsmen before Dexter were Peter May Colin Cowdrey and Tom Graveney.

May was the most majestic of the three, striding by right to the England captaincy in 1955, his career sadly shortened by illness in the early 1960s. He was discovered at Charterhouse by a famous pre-war England all-rounder, George Geary, and he became the most accomp-

Alec Bedser again – immaculate throughout his career.

lished batsman in the world after Bradman and Hutton. His cover-driving was a thing of splendour, but he had all the shots, and with his upright stance, broad shoulders and fast footwork was the most *satisfying* batsman to watch.

His partnership with Colin Cowdrey, against the West Indians at Edgbaston in 1957 – 411 – is still the world record Test partnership for the fourth wicket, and, in fact, the third-highest Test partnership ever. Cowdrey, one of England's most sterling cricketers for twenty years,

94

Colin Cowdrey. A battleship of a batsman.

was the complete batsman, with Hammond's ability to drive fast bowling and a fluent ease about his cricket that was a joy to watch. Even though he must have been the most completely *coached* cricketer almost since the day of his birth, when he was christened with the initials M.C.C. by a father with stars in his eyes, he always had, and still possesses, a deep love of the game and a sense of far greater meaning behind it. In his day he faced the finest fast bowlers in the world, Lindwall, Miller, Hall, Griffith, Lillee and Thomson. At the end of his career, at 42, he was called at little notice to fly to Australia to bolster Mike Denness' England side, both its openers out of action injured and the team shattered by Lillee and the new thunderbolt, Thomson. With just three days to acclimatise, he was pitched into the fray in the second Test at Perth, and batted at Number 3.

"It was challenging and stimulating cricket," he said. "Very much the way I had learned to bat with Peter May, the game so much more fulfilling." He played that lethal attack, with the ball lifting throat-high and higher from a good length on a bone-hard pitch, for 125 minutes for 22 runs, playing, as it were, from memory and instinct rather than with a genuine sense of seeing the ball. In the second innings he actually opened the innings, scoring 41, valiant as ever but, as he said, "we were well and truly beaten by fast bowling".

In his latter years Cowdrey seemed often inclined to drop into lower gear and succumb to the modern disease of waiting for "the right ball to hit". He was never a lightweight, even in his youth, and in his maturer years he began to resemble a ship in full sail. One of the nicer pieces of writing recently, indeed, came from John Woodcock, of *The Times*, who, describing Bob Woolmer, Kent and England successor to Cowdrey, got it exactly right: "Woolmer," he wrote, "is not unlike Cowdrey, as a cruiser is not unlike a battleship."

With this formidable pair the batting genius of Tom Graveney flowered fitfully during the 'fifties with Gloucestershire; and then in the 'sixties, after he had been dropped and neglected by the England selectors and discarded by Gloucestershire, he came to full maturity and fulfillment with Worcestershire and England. Everything about his batting was graceful. He began with an easy, upright stance, and a high backlift which at once made him slightly vulnerable to fast bowling early in his career and at the same time enabled him to launch the most handsome cover-drive in the business, with an equally high flourish on the followthrough. Of all the greater batsman, he was a front-foot player, using his height and reach (like Tony Greig) to move forward to the fast bowlers even when they were lifting. In defence he would play a half-cock shot off the front foot; and, to keep the score moving along if he was tied down, he developed this into a semi-push, semi-drive on

96

the rise. Once again his height enabled him usually to keep the ball down even when moving forward to the rising ball. And his reactions were so quick he was able to hook off the front foot, a stroke which in any less expert player would look like a cow-shot.

After Graveney and "Lord" Ted Dexter retired English batting had declined – so far as genuine style and character are concerned – and to the current jaundiced eye the batting crop of the 'seventies had been a mediocre one. Now, when we look back at the 'fifties and 'sixties, with the players we have mentioned and such fine performers as M. J. K. Smith, of Warwickshire, Reg Simpson of Nottinghamshire, Ken Barrington, it seemed that those were the "great old days". Just as in the 'fifties one looked back to Hammond and Hobbs, and in the 'thirties back to Fry and Jessop. But there are few players in the whole of the English scene today who, in all honesty, one can regard as genuine stylists.

Perhaps Boycott has a claim, with his great achievements and indomitable spirit, but surely the essence of a great batsman is that he can make the bowling look easy; Boycott, for all his merits, makes every ball except the rank long-hop or full-toss, look fearsomely difficult. His is the science of attrition, of concentration, but he has not yet found the flair to join the ranks of the really great, for all his achievements. No batsman ever let so many half-volleys go unpunished. Perhaps John Edrich, Bill's cousin, who reached his hundredth hundred in 1977, as did Boycott, and has played many a sterling innings for England and Surrey, might qualify, if only his bat had not performed so many limp and pawky gestures at the ball around off stump. Courage, yes, character, yes; style, no, not really. Bob Woolmer, the cruiser to Cowdrey's battleship, may make it one day when he has grown out of being a sound county player and matured into a fully-fledged Test batsman. Frank Hayes, when he is going well, shows glimpses of true style, as when he scored a century in his first Test match against the West Indians; but his lapses have been too great and too glaring. And Tony Greig, charismatic personality though he is, vast and spectacular though his cover-drive can be, is a crowd-puller because of what you hope he is going to do, rather than for any certainty that he will actually deliver. The only current batsman who to my mind qualifies to be added to the list of the stylists of cricket is Alan Knott, as we saw him at Nottingham against the Australians in 1977, impish, Comptonesque and dazzling in the array of his *attacking* strokes, backed by as straight a bat as you could hope to see when, occasionally, forced to defend.

Cause or effect? There is a strong school of thought that the importation of overseas stars into the county sides has lessened the chance of

The Late Cut

above: A. C. MacLaren dabs late and fine.

below: Jack Hobbs's cut was more a square slash.

above: Herbert Sutcliffe got right on top of the ball.

bottom left: Jack Robertson's was the wristiest of them all.

bottom right: And Neil Harvey, left-handed, could cut, like Denis Compton, off a good-length ball, so good was his eye and fast his reactions.

young English cricketers to make their names; or that potential stars have quit the game before even starting because their way to the top has been blocked. There is another school which says, with equal force, that the Kanhais, the Soberses, the Richardses (both of them), the Chappells, the Abbases, and the rest of the galaxy that has graced our grounds for so long, were in fact the saviours of cricket in this country; that the game was dying in the 'fifties until the overseas stars injected flair and brilliance into the sickly body, and that now, with that example before them, there are more potential youngsters in the pipeline than for years.

Players like Ian Botham, of Somerset, David Gower, of Leicestershire who have already made their mark on the Test scene, Athey of Yorkshire, Tavaré and Cowdrey Junior of Kent, Gatting of Middlesex, Hopkins of Glamorgan and my son, Paul, of Sussex, are knocking on the door of greatness; and about the only major benefit to the game likely to come out of the whole unsavoury mess of the Kerry Packer affair is that some of these youngsters may well get their chance to prove themselves sooner than otherwise might have been the case.

The awful gap left by the war in England's bowling ranks, particularly among the opening bowlers, was filled for seven years and more by that genial and often misunderstood giant, Alec Bedser. It was said of him at the time that he was so dominant at his craft that it sometimes appeared that he was bowling from both ends at once.

From the beginning of his career, Alec Bedser was a "natural". He had an inherent inswing, which he found by experimentation that he could make move very late. But he realised that this stock ball of his needed to be varied, and he developed a lethal outswinger and "legcutter" – "Barnes's ball" – that took him several hundreds of wickets. He found that his best and most comfortable run-up was of only seven paces, and with his fine build he was able to bowl for hour after hour on all types of pitches. Sometimes it was said that his arm came over lower than it should do, but that usually was part of the variation in his bowling, for he was a master of subtlety. He also studied his subject in minute detail, and playing against the great Bradman, he developed a refinement of the leg theory (not to be confused in any way with bodyline) which on several occasions trapped the great man into being kept unusually quiet and eventually to being caught by leg-slip.

In all, in his career, he took over 1900 wickets, and was one of the prime reasons why Surrey established an unbreakable hold over the County Championships under the enthusiastic captaincy of Stuart Surridge. But in his Test career, he was too often unsupported, either by his fellow-bowlers or the batsmen. Time and again Bedser would breach the other side's defences, with 5, 6 or 7 wickets, only to find the advantage thrown away by poor fielding, loose bowling and spineless batting. So his 236 Test wickets at a time when English cricket was at its lowest ebb not only were remarkable in themselves, but also a mark of a man with a very great heart. Now, as chairman of the England selectors, he has helped take English cricket out of the doldrums once more, picking the team which has battled through the storm of yet another great pair of Australian fast bowlers to regain the Ashes.

From rags to riches in cricket takes but a little time, just as the opposite journey can also be a matter of an aeroplane ride away, as the Australian team found in 1977. And the grey days of the 'forties gave way to the opulence of the 'fifties when England's batting strength of Hutton, May, Cowdrey and Graveney was spearheaded by the best fast bowling combinations of the decade; and were the pace men to fail, then there was that amazing Surrey duo, Jim Laker and Tony Lock, to bamboozle the opposition with right- and left-arm spin.

But first, the "quickies". Statham and Tyson; Statham and Trueman. For seven years or more Brian Statham formed the basis of the England fast attack while his more mercurial partners took the limelight. His first-class career lasted eighteen years and in that time he took 2260 wickets at an average of 16.36. Freddie Trueman, in two years longer, took 2304 wickets, averaging 18.29. Statham, from Lancashire, was smooth-striding, consistently very fast-medium, and attacked the wickets all the time. His were the prime virtues of line and length, consistency and accuracy. If you got away from the thunderbolts of Trueman, there was no relief, for the penetrating accuracy and Statham at the other end could, and would, search out the batsman's weakness and take advantage of his every lapse in concentration. Statham rarely used the bumper, but when he did, it was a brute, and his fast off-break, which nipped in from the pitch, was lethal. He was often regarded as almost too accurate, but he played in 70 Tests, more than any other fast bowler, and took 252 wickets, despite shaving the stumps unsuccessfully more often than not.

From across the Pennines and up from the coalmines came Fred Trueman, big, black-haired and menacing. He would bowl himself to a standstill, bump the ball all day, thrust at and intimidate batsmen with his huge black glare, his appeal a clap of thunder, his scowl for the unco-operative umpire a glare of menace. He was the most rumbustious, cantankerous, cussed personality on the whole of the cricket circuit, and the crowds loved him. His first ball against the Australian team of 1953 was a bumper to Hassett, at The Oval, and the crowd buzzed as, at last, they felt that the years of painful and bruising frustration at the hands of Lindwall and Miller were coming to an end. (The feeling was identical in 1977 when Willis was whistling the ball

Brian Statham. As accurate as Barnes. Batsmen used to "escape" from Statham only to find themselves up against Tyson or Trueman.

around the ears of Chappell and his ineffectual team.) Trueman went on to take 307 Test wickets, including one devastating spell of 5 wickets in 27 balls without conceding a run against the Australians at Headingley in 1961, shortening his run and bowling cutters into worn patches on the pitch.

Colin Cowdrey, in his warm autobiography, tells the story of how Trueman came to the magic figure of 300 wickets. Trueman, with 297 wickets to his credit, had begun to run out of steam, but had been recalled for the Oval Test of 1964. Ted Dexter was the captain, and "Fiery Fred", although he bowled reasonably well, had no luck, and was taken off. He retired to short leg, muttering.

"At this point England got stuck. We had begun the morning well but in the half-hour before lunch we were bogged down again and Dexter was beginning to look as desperate as Trueman. He came in from the covers at the end of an over tossing the ball from hand to hand, and as we met at the middle of the pitch he simply said 'We must try something different, any ideas?' Whatever plans he had in his mind, only one thing was certain. None of them included bringing back Trueman.

"For once, however, Dexter was over-ruled. Before I had time to answer his question a frantic voice just behind me said: 'I'm going to bowl.' It was Freddie Trueman about to prove that possession is ten-tenths of the law. For as Dexter said, 'Wait a moment, Freddie', Trueman snatched the ball from his captain's hand and began striding away towards the sightscreen to begin his run. Short of actually starting a punch-up in the very centre of a Test pitch, Dexter was nonplussed. He chuckled away, walked out to cover point and accepted the situation for the next six balls. It may not have been orthodox captaincy but in this instance it proved to be wise. After all, if your leading bowler, a great one at that, wants to bowl, why stop him?

"Trueman's first three deliveries can only be described as wildly inaccurate. But with the last two he saved himself. They were just enough on target to earn him another over, the last before lunch, without any real argument. And it was in that over that he knocked out Redpath's middle stump and, with the very next ball, had McKenzie flashing at a ball that I held at slip . . ."

After a tense lunch, or rather no lunch at all for the prowling Trueman, Neil Hawke prevented the hat-trick, but "for the next fifteen minutes Trueman bowled with real inspiration. He was perhaps not quite so fast as he had been at the peak of his career, but all the skill and fire came flooding back and he was a wonderful sight to watch. It was as though he felt this was his final act in Test cricket and he was determined to leave an indelible memory of his prowess. Ironically the wicket took some time coming, but this time Trueman took a firm control on his frustration and at last Hawke snicked a catch to me at slip. It was straightforward, but sharp, coming firmly at a good height just to my right, and I took it comfortably. But easy or not it was several minutes before my heart resumed its normal pace. It would have been on my conscience for the rest of my days had I dropped that catch on the day Freddie Trueman hi-jacked the England bowling."

Bill Bowes, Yorkshire and England bowler himself of tremendous merit, describes Trueman's style better than anyone. In a tribute in *Wisden* in 1970, he wrote: "He showed up mediocrity in an opponent in a manner no other bowler of his time could equal. He had a flair, as any cricketer of top rank must have, for being able to perform above expectations, 'above himself' as it is generally put. In a couple of overs Trueman could transform the whole outlook of a game. Sometimes it was a fluky shot through the slips, sometimes a stroke of copybook perfection that produced the spark that fired him. Sometimes it was for no other reason that it was time somebody got somewhere. A pitch, at one moment docile and easy-paced, would suddenly become possessed of every kind of devil.

". . . He was a tremendous talker. . . . He was never silent " except during his actual run-up to bowl and in the delivery action; it would have been a pity if anything had marred this beautiful, sometimes awe-inspiring sight. He ran the length of another cricket pitch to bowl. Some critics said he ran much too far, but Trueman said he felt better that way.

"This was the perfect answer and it meant much more than the opinion of Ranjitsinhji, who thought all fast bowlers should take a long run because the longer periods of concentration required from the batsmen had a telling effect. There was a tendency for the concentration to wander.

"With sweet gathering of momentum Freddie, black hair waving, came hurtling to the bowling crease. With no change of rhythm there came the change from forward to sideways motion, the powerful gathering of muscles for the delivery itself, and then the 'explosive' release. A perfect cartwheel action, with every spoke of arms and legs pointing to where the ball was to go – the batsman seeing nothing but left shoulder prior to the moment of delivery – gave the ball its 90 mph propulsion. There was the full-blooded follow-through to the action, a run through while he braked, which worried umpires if he got too near the line of the stumps, and then, a hundred to one, more talk. . . ."

For a couple of seasons in the mid-fifties Frank Tyson, the "Typhoon", took all the headlines, being mainly responsible for England's holding the Ashes in Hutton's tour of 1954–55. Faster than Miller, Lindwall, Trueman or Statham, he relied on sheer speed to make

"Fiery Fred" Trueman. He'd bowl a bouncer off a one-pace run, if needed.

Frank Tyson – the "Typhoon" called up by Hutton to shatter the Aussies.

106

his effect. He was almost unknown when the selectors, on a mere jot or tittle of evidence, sent him on that tour; and when he took only 1 wicket for 160 in the first Test it seemed as though the gamble had failed. But, under Hutton's guidance, Tyson trained furiously, cut down his run without losing his speed, and in the second Test at Sydney he took in all 10 wickets for 130. Apart from the brilliant left-hander, Neil Harvey, who hit 92 not out, no-one could handle the tall, strong Northamptonshire man's expresses. In the first innings he took 4 for 45; and then, when he batted, he turned his back on a retaliatory bouncer from Lindwall and was felled by a blow on the back of the head. You could see the bump from the boundary. When Australia set about getting the 223 needed for victory, he took 6 for 85 and bowled England to victory. Lindwall was one of his victims, yorked as he backed away from the stumps (shades of Larwood). And so the tour went on, Tyson's thunderbolts leaving the Australians wrecked and floundering as if swept aside by a gale.

There is an interesting sidelight both on Tyson's bowling and Hutton's captaincy in Cowdrey's book, and another echo of Larwood's day.

"Hutton's target was Richie Benaud. Carefully filed away in his mind was the memory of Benaud in trouble against Tyson's bowling. Benaud came in apparently to face the bowling of Johnny Wardle, a hope which Hutton actively encouraged with an expression of bland absent-mindedness. He actually let Wardle take the ball, set his field and turned to run in before he called out 'Oh, hold on a minute, hold on.' Then followed an extraordinary act of pretending not to know where Tyson was fielding. He peered everyhere before finally looking down to third man where he knew damned well Tyson would be, and then went into an elaborate rigmarole of calling him up from the distant boundary, taking the ball from Wardle and handing it to Tyson with a long, whispered conversation. The build-up was nerve-wracking. Benaud watched and waited anxiously, a tactic which he used from time to time in his days as captain. Hutton used variations on that theme against Benaud practically every time he came into bat throughout the entire series. Whoever was bowling at the time, Tyson would be summoned up to take over, even if he were on his knees with exhaustion. The tactic did not work at Sydney, but on three other occasions it was Tyson who got Benaud out. It conjured up the picture of Jardine's similar use of Larwood against Bradman twenty-two years ago on these same grounds."

Tyson's career was shortened when his ankles gave out under the strain of bowling so fast on rock-hard pitches. But he left behind a number of bruised and broken batsmen and the memory of his shuffling launch, giant strides and delivery action in which the back was

On the follow-through

top left: Keith Miller – very fast in short bursts.
top right: Wes Hall – genuine pace from the West Indies.

Dennis Lillee – lost to Packer, but still a great bowler.

*Michael Holding –
power and beauty in
action.*

*Andy Roberts –
moody and
magnificent fast
bowler.*

used like a steel spring – and speed, sheer speed.

He thoroughly enjoyed bowling fast. In his autobiography, written after he settled (like Larwood) in Australia when his career was over, he wrote: "Oh, yes, there have been better fast bowlers, but I doubt whether there has been one who derived more pleasure from bowling fast. One of its great attractions for me is its straightforwardness. It is an honest pursuit whose rewards are gained by the sweat of the brow, not by any underhand or surreptitious methods."

After this formidable trio, England have been hard put to it to find one genuine fast bowler, let alone a pair. John Snow, of Sussex, soldiered on moodily and occasionally magnificently for England (as his 200 Test wickets prove). With his fine physique, long rhythmic run-up with the right arm held low, his fluent delivery and menacing follow-through, he looked every inch the part. But Snow, the only fast bowler I know to have a book of his own poems published, could also lose interest too quickly in a game, and was often in trouble with the (still strait-laced) authorities at Lord's for his outspokenness and his addition to minor peccadilloes, like wearing advertising matter on his clothes and swearing at the umpire.

With good reason, there was widespread criticism when the selectors left him out of the 1974–75 tour of Australia. True, by then he was perhaps past his best, but he was the only English bowler who could have answered the thunderbolts of Thomson and Lillee with a like barrage. He was always hostile, his bouncers had every Australian batsman of his time in trouble, and he had a beautiful outswinger that moved late from the bat.

With him, Geoff Arnold of Surrey was a successful swing bowler with genuine style. I saw him bowl the most professional over against Turner, the New Zealander who made 1000 runs in May, in the spring of 1973. Fresh from this triumph, Turner opened the batting in the Lord's Test match full of confidence. Arnold bowled him five consecutive inswingers, all on a length, all coming from off stump to leg stump and forcing Turner to play every one, which he did, with an immaculate forward defensive prod. A penny piece, new or old, would have covered the spot on the pitch where every ball pitched. The sixth ball was a late outswinger which pitched on the same spot and moved away just enough to touch the outside edge of the defensive bat and carry through for a straightforward slip catch. It was swing bowling at its best, and Arnold knew how to use English conditions as well as Bedser himself.

Of England's modern bowlers, Bob Willis is the most hostile, with Mike Hendrick and Chris Old, and left-arm swinger John Lever, the pick of the bunch. Willis seems to have got over the leg and knee injury

110

A modern stylist. Mike Hendrick's action is as near poetry in motion as anyone's in cricket today.

problems which dogged his early career – perhaps because he has smoothed out his action without sacrificing pace, straightened his curving, high-kneed run, and bangs the ball down onto the pitch from the full height of a very long arm. Mike Hendrick, a "thinking" bowler after the Bedser style, is no more than fast-medium, but he too can swing the ball either way and his leg-cutter is usually bowled to a very full length off an easy run-up. He can bowl all day, and has the heart to do so too. Chris Old, who often looks the most innocuous of the three, has the knack of taking wickets with what apparently are straightfor-

111

ward balls, but he too does a little in the air and off the pitch, and has greatly improved his accuracy and consistency. If he can get over his dislike of facing very fast bowling, he looks like being an England all-rounder for a very long time, for he is a superb hard-hitting batsman, who has already hit a century in 37 minutes, only two minutes slower than Percy Fender's fastest-ever.

★　　★　　★　　★　　★

Possibly because of the l.b.w. law in operation since the mid-1930s, in England, at least, the old right-arm leg-break and googly bowler has practically died out. In recent years the accent has always been on accuracy, particularly in the one-day games that have done so much to revitalise cricket. It is always argued that the "wrist-spinner" – the man who turns his wrist and rolls the ball out of the back of his hand – is of necessity less accurate than the orthodox off-spinner, who spins, or cuts the ball with his fingers in order to get it to move in the air and off the pitch. I wonder what Mailey, Grimmett and O'Reilly, Charlie Parker and Tich Freeman and Doug Wright would do in modern cricket. Certainly the last English leg-spinner of note and class was Robin Hobbs, who played for England seven times without great success in 1967–68 but, many people believe, was never really given a long-running chance because leg-spin has been out of fashion for the past twenty years. Australia's Richie Benaud, who would have found an Australian Test place as a batsman alone, with a superb leg-spinner in the best tradition, with an immaculate, sideways-on action with a high, rolling arm. But since he retired to become a television commentator, the best-known in the world, Australia have not found anyone to replace him, although to their credit the selectors have (unlike England's) never ceased trying.

D. V. P. Wright, of Kent, was generally reckoned the unluckiest bowler of all. He bowled leg-breaks off a fast-bowler's run, and he bowled them very much faster than anyone else. He was a genuine match-winner who never quite fulfilled his potential, although he stands alone in the records as having taken seven hat-tricks in his career. He took over 2000 wickets, more than 100 of them in Tests, and in the years just after the war he took the brunt of the spin attack for England, as Bedser did with pace.

But it was an off-spinner who performed the most astounding feat of the mid-fifties or any other era – Jim Laker.

Laker, who was born in Yorkshire, but settled down in the South to play for Surrey, announced his presence to the cricket world in 1950 (although he'd toured West Indies with MCC a couple of years before) with the (then) best bowling performance in all first-class cricket. In

112

Jim Laker – the greatest off-spinner of any age or any country.

the Test trial of that year his figures were: 14 overs, 12 maidens, 2 runs, 8 wickets. He was unplayable, and wrecked the trial.

Six years later, of course, twice in one year he took all 10 Australian wickets in an innings – for Surrey and for England; and in the Manchester Test match he had the incredible figures of 19 wickets for 90 runs – an average that theoretically can be surpassed: but such lightning surely can't strike more than once in one lifetime, and Jim Laker is still very much alive and well and commentating for the BBC.

Laker used the orthodox off-spinner's method, bowling off a short run-up with his right arm held high in front of his face, spinning the ball primarily with the forefinger. He bowled at a fair pace, although not as fast as, say, Underwood, but with great control over length and direction. On a rain-affected or crumbling pitch, he could make the ball "talk", lifting viciously and turning almost at right angles. On this type of wicket he invariably ringed the bat with fieldsmen, using three short legs – one at leg slip, one short square, and one forward short.

With Tony Lock, his Surrey partner, spinning left-arm from the other end, they were a menacing pair to meet indeed.

Thanks to the dominance of the Surrey twins, few other spinners got much of a look-in, but for years Jack Young, of Middlesex, was one of the foremost practitioners of orthodox left-arm spin, with a flowing run-up and, using varying length and pace, one that "went with the arm". Since Laker's day, the supply of off-spinners proliferated, with David Allen, Bob Appleyard, Ray Illingworth, Freddie Titmus, Pat Pocock and now John Emburey, of Middlesex, who in one full season of county cricket played himself into England reckoning. The mantle of left-arm tradition has fallen on the modest shoulders of Derek Underwood, who is known by friend and foe alike as "Deadly". I am told it is due to the quality of his jokes in the dressing-room, but as the seasons roll on his bowling has more than justified the *nom de guerre*. He is perhaps slightly faster than most slow bowlers, and indeed his quicker ball approaches medium-pace. He takes a longish run-up, to settle his rhythm, and delivers every ball with precisely the same action. His wrist is held low, concealing the ball from the batsman as he runs up, in the manner of a chinaman bowler, but he cocks it at the last moment before delivery, and his stock ball is the orthodox left-hander's leg-break to the right-hander. He will bowl this ball for over after over, varying the flight and spin to keep the batsman worried, and, just as the unfortunate man has decided he has the measure of Underwood, along comes the fast one that goes to leg with the arm and nips through to bowl him, or trap him l.b.w. In his earlier days, Underwood tended to bowl too fast, even on helpful pitches, and was sometimes accused of "playing the batsman in". But of late, particularly in the

114

1977 series against Australia, he has varied his pace more, given the ball air, and become a more lethal bowler as a result. His main virtue is his nagging accuracy. He is capable of keeping the strongest batsman under control for long periods of time; and many a wicket has accrued to Kent and England from the batsman's trying to unload his frustration on whoever is Underwood's partner at the time.

Don Bradman's all-conquering side immediately after the war was packed with all-round strength. If he faltered, which he did occasionally if only to prove that he was human after all, there were Bill Brown, Sid Barnes, Lindsay Hassett, the mercurial Keith Miller (who made it almost a principle to begin tours of England by scoring a double-century), and one of the most brilliant left-handers of all time, Neil Harvey, to fall back on. But the real difference in the sides lay, as it did after the First World War, with his bowling strength. He had Miller and Lindwall, a match in every way for the formidable Gregory and McDonald who carved their way through J. W. H. T. Douglas's teams in the early 'twenties.

Keith Miller was the most reluctant bowler of all – indeed, he missed one tour of South Africa because he let it be known that he only wanted to be considered as a batsman. But with Lindwall operating at the other end, he was devastating. At one time he hoped to be a jockey, because he was so small, but (a curious fact in common with many other great cricketers, like Clive Lloyd, Tony Greig and Graeme Pollock) between the ages of 16 and 17 he suddenly shot up over a foot and, although he retained his love of racing, an active career in the sport was out of the question. Miller always professed a couldn't-careless attitude to his cricket, but underneath was a ruthless and sometimes selfish determination to succeed. He developed into one of the finest all-rounders the game has known, with his cavalier batting, his ability to bowl off any length of run, and his often deceptively casual catching in the slips. Bradman and Lindsay Hassett and Ian Johnson after him were all accused at one time after another of bowling Miller too much, so that it affected his batting. However, in 55 Tests he collected just under 3000 runs and 170 wickets, although Miller himself was as unlikely to have added them up as any cricketer who ever lived. If he had bothered to fight as hard at uncritical moments as he always did when the chips were down, his figures would be even more formidable. He was incapable of dullness, and cricket took on a new look when he was on view. (Derek Randall and Alan Knott have that capability as batsmen.) But in spite of that, it was as a fast bowler he will be more remembered, in harness with Lindwall.

Ray Lindwall (although he could bat too, most effectively on occasions) was totally different in personality. He was primarily a cricke-

The Sweep
Len Hutton's style and grace transformed even a clumsy shot.

Denis Compton made the stroke something of a trade-mark.

Frank Worrell's sweep, like Hammond's, was performed off one knee.

ter's cricketer, with an old-fashioned approach to the game. Cartoonists could make little of him, and neither could many batsmen, for he appeared one of the least alarming of fast bowlers – until you faced him. He carefully preserved his fitness. He rarely began a spell of bowling without going through a spell of flexing the muscles of his back and legs – as Alan Knott does today – and he never attempted any action beyond the limit of his poise and control, which were extensive. His run-up was leisurely, its smoothness concealing the subtle increase in pace to the moment of delivery. He stooped somewhat, in obedience to Spofforth's principles enunciated so clearly 80 years before, and although his delivery stride was long, he did not leap into it like Gregory or Hall. He had a marked drag with the right toes, and – most obvious of all – he brought his arm over wide, fully stretched from beginning to end. It was this that prompted several observers to dub him non-classical, but he had complete control over line, length and pace, and in this respect most nearly resembled Harold Larwood. If he wanted to bowl a yorker, he did so. If he wanted to bowl a bumper, there it was, not rising so sharply as Miller's from the height of his arm, but disturbing and uncomfortable to the batsman's dignity.

In 61 Tests for Australia, he took 228 wickets at an average of 23.05 – figures exceeded only by Richie Benaud and Graham McKenzie. He was no mean batsman, either, scoring 1502 Test runs for his country, including two centuries.

Of the batsmen, Arthur Morris was probably the most elegant left-hander since Woolley, in direct line from Clem Hill to Neil Harvey. He and Barnes and Miller all averaged over 70 in the 1948 Tests. Barnes was a massive scorer – and so too was Hassett.

In that series, Neil Harvey, at the time only nineteen, played his first Test match against England, and scored the first of his 21 Test centuries in a career which was to span the next fifteen years. Many Australian batsmen have had the misfortune to be dubbed the "second Bradman", which is a sad label to tag onto anybody and has hung with the weight of an albatross round the necks of Ian Craig, Norman O'Neill and Doug Walters, to name but three. But Harvey, although he batted left-handed, could stand with Bradman in any reckoning. He was fairly short and compact, like Bradman, and his left-handed genius lit up cricket grounds all over the world. He had all the shots, particularly on the off side, and he had to a degree the great batsman's ability to see the ball early and change his shot if necessary. For many years, too, he was a quicksilver cover point, second only to Bland of his time. In all Tests he scored over 6000 runs for an average of 48.41, again, second only to Bradman.

Australian cricket, and that of most of the world, was dominated for a long spell in the 'fifties by Richie Benaud, who not only took more Test wickets than any other Australian (248) but scored over 2000 Test runs. Benaud, though, will be remembered more for his classic leg-spin and googly bowling than for his batting, forceful though it was. He was also a shrewd and inspiring captain for Australia, and has turned into the most knowledgeable television commentator on the game. Sometimes it is almost as if he had a personal wire to the fielding skipper, for if Richie says "He ought to bring on so-and-so now – that batsman is looking unsafe outside the off stump" or some such remark, then it is a pound to a pinch of snuff that the captain will bring on so-and-so for the next over. Benaud, it might be said, is the last really great leg-spinner to have played for any country apart possibly from Chandrasekhar of India, but it is to be hoped that the pendulum will swing again, as it has so often in cricket, and we shall see this most attractive and (on the right wicket) deadly form of bowling in action again.

Benaud was followed as skipper of Australia by Bobby Simpson, another great amasser of runs who also bowled leg-breaks, but by no means as well as Benaud; and then came one of the most extraordinary figures – left-hander Bill Lawry. He was not an extraordinary strokemaker, but a run-accumulator extraordinary, who began by wearing the opposition bowling down by playing a straight bat, nearly always off the front foot, for hour after hour without ever trying to make a scoring stroke. Then he would break loose, hitting particularly hard on the leg side. He had the left-hander's pull to perfection.

He took his stance with his back slightly arched over the bat, his long nose pointing down the wicket, and always his initial movement was a shuffle onto the short foot. His backswing was short to meet the swinging ball, and he clipped rather than smote the ball through the off-side field. He watched every ball right onto the bat, and hooked and slashed fearlessly off his nose, eyebrows or wherever else the bowler happened to aim the ball. He averaged more than 50 runs an innings in Test matches, establishing himself as one of the great opening batsmen of the century. Clem Hill, his spiritual ancestor, would have been proud of him. And he proved an astute and successful captain.

In the meantime, Australia had been hard put to it to fill the gap at the top of the attack left when Lindwall and Miller eventually faded out. For some time Alan Davidson, fast left-hander and good batsman too, battled on with a series of assistants, one of whom, Ian Meckiff, was removed from the lists after long and strong accusations of throwing – not before he had won a Test series or two, however. For nearly the whole of the 'sixties, a genial giant, Graham McKenzie, held sway with an easy, rolling action like Maurice Tate's, and he finished with a bag of 246 Test wickets – only 2 fewer than the great Benaud himself.

But it was not until 1974, when Dennis Lillee was joined by Jeff Thomson, that Australia once again found the opening attack that was to blast their country back to the top of the cricket heap. Between them they destroyed England in Australia in 1974–75, then enabled Australia to hold the Ashes in the four-match tour of England in the following summer; then home again in 1975–76 they completely shattered the West Indian claim to be champions of the world.

Lillee had already proved a fine fast bowler in the 1972 series against England, finishing with 31 wickets in the five Tests, including 10 in the last, which was won by Australia to level the series. On the following tour to West Indies, his back, which had been worrying him, broke down completely, and he was found to have three stress fractures at the base of the spine. He was in great pain, and it was thought that he would never play again. But after an operation, with amazing patience and determination, he fought his way back to peak fitness, and turned out in 1974–75 to face the England team in harness with Thomson, having improved in accuracy and now bowling possibly even quicker than he had been before. He is a most menacing bowler, particularly with his Zapata moustache, breathing fire and fury in a long, straight, springy run and an immaculate delivery. His follow through is as furious as ever was Trueman's, and his appeal is not so much a question to the umpire as a challenge to the gods, often made on his knees. Like Larwood and Lindwall, he has fine control over his length and swing and pace, and although his slower ball is not always so well disguised, it often takes wickets in the batsman's relief and intention at least to hit the cover off *that* one. His breakback, when it comes, like Thomson's, is almost unplayable, and he is a fearsome exponent of the bouncer.

Derek Randall, who has both failed and succeeded against Lillee and Thomson, infuriated Lillee during the famous Centenary Test at Melbourne in March 1977. Lillee hit him on the ankle with a ball that cut back, and ended his follow through within a couple of yards of Randall, his arms outstretched in raucous appeal. As he glared at Randall, the young Nottinghamshire batsman told him, coolly: "If you can't bounce 'em higher than that, Dennis, you can't be that good." The next ball reared off just short of a length, caught Randall on the head, and knocked him down. Randall said later: "If he'd hit me anywhere else, it'd have killed me." And then he went on to make an historic 174. But Lillee had the last laugh, winning the match for Australia by 45 runs in a superb exhibition of fast bowling.

There is no doubt in my mind that Lillee is in a far higher class than "Thommo" as a fast bowler, and fit to rank with any of the greats of the past. He is a genuine cricketer, superbly athletic and with a will to win second to none.

120

Thomson still has to mature as a fast bowler and a cricketer, but he is undeniably fast. At Perth, during the West Indian tour, he was timed by photosonic camera equipment at 99.688 mph, with Roberts at 93.6 mph, Holding 92.3 mph and Lillee 86.4 mph, but according to Tommy Penrose, the senior lecturer in physical education at the Western Australian University, the tests should not be regarded as conclusive. He bowls off a shorter run than Lillee, for he gets his power from a V-shaped back and a slinging action that requires a curious "chassée" with the right leg crossing behind the left in the stride before delivery. But the back is arched like a bow and the hand, which has swung down behind him at full stretch, is brought over in a perfect arc. David's slingshot that slew Goliath could have generated no greater velocity.

But on the 1977 tour of England, with Lillee retired from cricket to preserve his health for later years (or, the cynical said, for Kerry Packer) Thomson was a shadow of his former self. He had suffered a collision in the field the previous December, going for a catch, and severely dislocated his shoulder. Although the Australian camp put out that "Thommo's" shoulder was perfectly fit, and he performed gallantly during the whole series, he was never more than a shadow of the man who had terrorised the English batsmen two years before.

In 1974, Dennis Lillee published an autobiography which he's never retracted, saying, in part: "I try to hit a batsman in the rib cage when I bowl a purposeful bouncer, and I want it to hurt so much that the batsman doesn't want to face me any more." That, and Thomson's own quote in which he has stated that he "enjoyed hitting a batsman more than getting him out" have caused cricket authorities to look closely at the rules about intimidating bowling; but in spite of all the blurb, I believe that England were intimidated only by sheer speed in those two series. Colin Cowdrey, called on to stop the gap after Amiss and Edrich were both injured, seems to indicate this also in his own book *M.C.C.*, as we have seen earlier (p 103).

No whining there.

*   *   *   *   *

In recent years one generation of Australian batsmen has come and gone, and now Australia are in the throes of building their side afresh. Ian Redpath, a superb opening batsman and one of the best Australian players of slow bowling, has put his bat away; Doug Walters, who on his day and on a good wicket could look one of the world's best batsmen (and always was one of the world's best fielders), is near the end of a career which was marred only by the fact that he never really came off on English wickets; the lovely stroke-master Keith Stackpole, who

Note the position of the head in both these wonderful hits for six. Like a golfer's the eyes are fixed on where the ball was – not where they hope it's going to be.

Frank Worrell, hitting himself and his country into the history books during his 261 against England in 1950.

122

Garfield Sobers, without doubt the greatest all-rounder the world has known since "W. G.", during his "farewell" century at Lord's in 1974.

hooked harder than most, has retired; the immaculate Paul Sheahan has become a schoolmaster; and the Chappell brothers, known the cricket world over as the Chafia (after the Mafia), have joined the Packer camp.

Ian Chappell, the older brother, was one of Australia's toughest captains and second-best batsmen of the decade. (His brother Greg is a more elegant, stylish player.) He scored 5187 runs for his country in Tests, averaging 42.86, and he retired after scoring 196, his highest Test innings, against England at The Oval in 1975. He played every game as hard as he knew how, and he was respected and feared as a batsman and captain all over the world. Greg Chappell was more aloof, less abrasive than Ian, who could antagonise anyone at the drop of a four-letter word, but Greg's upright, classical stance (compare it with C. B. Fry's, Vivian Richards's or Archie MacLaren's) was the basis of some of the most classical batsmanship you could hope to see. He, more than any other batsman I have seen, could judge to a fraction of an inch which ball to leave, which to play. He was master of the crease from the moment he took guard. His cover-driving was in Hammond class and his timing off his toes to leg equalled the best in our time. His batting suffered from the strain of captaincy in England in 1977, with the shadow of Kerry Packer hanging over the series like a large black cloud, and yet it was always a surprise when Greg Chappell was dismissed for a few runs. More than any other batsman, he looked good for a century every time he went in to bat. In fact he hit 12 Test centuries in 70 Test innings – an average of one every six times at the wicket. As a captain he had one marvellous series against West Indies, and one bad one against England. It seemed that when things were going right for him, he was a good skipper, but he was not so firm or authoritative as his brother when the odds turned against him. In that series, even his slip-catching let him, and Australia, down. And it had never done that before.

On that tour, indeed, every reputation suffered, except possibly those of the valiant Max Walker and, after a poor start, Rick McCosker. But in different circumstances, English crowds might have seen and appreciated more of the talents of young batsmen like Hughes, Serjeant, Hookes and Cosier. Perm any three from those four and you have the stars of the future.

6
Recent History

While English cricket stuttered along in fits and starts after the last war, years of glory interspersed with longer periods of mediocrity, and the game in Australia was proceeding on a more even course, with more highs than lows, the influence of West Indies has been steadily increasing; and it surely must not be long now before they genuinely can claim to be world champions. The supply of talent seems to be everlasting, even if some of their most gifted players burn themselves out through over-enthusiasm and find themselves forced into early retirement – like Keith Boyce – by persistent muscle or tendon injuries. But of all the galaxy of stars which have come to invade English cricket since the war the West Indians have been the most consistently successful and exciting. In the era in which the bulk of the local talent has appeared at best pedestrian, the stimulus of West Indian many-splendoured gifts has been both the saviour of and an inspiration to the game in England. This is not to deny the contribution made by South Africans like Barry Richards and Mike Procter; or Indians and Pakistanis of the calibre of Bishan Bedi, Zaheer Abbas and Majid Khan; or of Glenn Turner, the New Zealander.

To see West Indian cricket at its best is to see it in West Indies. In the grey drab of the average English summer, or on the hot, hard soulless pitches of Melbourne and Sydney, some of the virtue goes out of it. West Indies has been the melting pot of the world's civilisations over the centuries, and its people are the most beautiful you will ever meet anywhere. They have volatile temperaments, and they have always tended to play their cricket in the same way as they live their lives. They are happy, excitable and flamboyant and their approach to cricket has captured the imagination in a way that no other nation has done.

To attend a Test match at the Queen's Park Oval in Port of Spain, or at Sabina Park in Kingston, is to experience the gamut of emotions possible to human beings, from riotous rage to unbelievable ecstasy, from vast good humour to unbridled fury. The West Indians learned years ago, unlike England's reluctant football clubs, to confine their more excitable spectators behind stout wire-mesh. Even so, the incorrigibles still clamber over to play tag with the riot squad, chasing vainly across the outfield brandishing white riots sticks and clutching absurd white helmets the while. The crowd cheers on the escaping miscreant as he scrambles over the wire in a flash, to be absorbed in a mass of black faces and grinning white teeth. Outside the 20-foot walls the boys build human ladders, clambering onto each other's shoulders to nip over the top, then hanging head-down to haul up their brothers from down below. Every palm-tree holds a score or more of spectators, growing little black coconuts among the fronds, and every vantage point for half a mile round the ground is festooned with spectators. Nowhere in the city need one be out of touch, for every West Indian has a transistor set pressed to his ear, and ball-by-ball accounts surge along the crowded streets.

But for all their exciting and compelling characteristics, West Indies did not really become a world cricketing force until their players had learned to discipline themselves to the harsh demands of Test cricket. This moment arrived in 1950 when, headed by a new pair of bowling "twins", Ramadhin and Valentine, and backed by the three Ws, they spun England's batsmen out as the three Ws thumped the English bowlers into decline. The West Indian side of that year, under the captaincy of John Goddard, of Barbados, was probably the best-balanced team that had ever been chosen, but they did not know that when they started out. Neither tiny Sonny Ramadhin, from Trinidad, nor Alfred Valentine, both nineteen, had ever played in a first-class match before, except for a Test trial. Yet they proved to be the best spin-bowling combination seen since before the war, and a calypso was written for them which became a best seller.

Ramadhin was very small, with tiny hands and feet, but it was years before English or Australian batsmen really sorted out his spin. He was a mystery bowler whose stock ball was supposed to be the off-spinner; but the mystery stemmed from the unorthodox way he held the ball. When bowling the off-break he spun the ball with his *second* finger (in place of the usual forefinger); and when bowling his leg-break, he did not change his grip. On English wickets particularly he could spin the ball a great deal, and he was virtually unplayable in 1950 and remained so until Peter May and Colin Cowdrey took him apart in a record stand of 411 for the fourth wicket at Edgbaston in 1957.

His partner, Valentine, a tall, lugubrious left-hander, probably spun the ball more than any non-wrist-spinner playing. He had long, strong fingers, and his jerky action put an amazing amount of body into each delivery; and when he went to Australia in 1951–52 they called him "Young Man River" because he just kept bowling along.

126

The three Ws – Frank Worrell, Everton Weekes and Clyde Walcott, came together after the war, all from Barbados. In 1945–46 Worrell and Walcott put on 574 without being defeated against Trinidad, which stands as the second-highest partnership recorded in first-class cricket. They were all great batsmen – Weekes possibly the most devastating, with steel wrists and a tremendous hook-cum-sweep shot that Rohan Kanhai perfected in later years, in which the batsman turned full circle with the power of the shot, frequently landing up on his backside. Clyde Walcott was possibly the most adventurous, thrashing the ball all round the wicket. But Worrell was the most elegant and orthodox of the three. His self-taught technique was so correct that he seemed incapable of playing a crooked stroke. Lithely built and superbly balanced, he was a stylist with an unhurried air, although his wide range of strokes, off front or back foot, was based on early and rapid movement into the correct position. His cutting was delicate, his driving easy and powerful, and he was strong on both sides of the wicket. He was at first a left-arm slow bowler, but a couple of seasons in Lancashire League cricket turned him into fast-medium, with a sharp lift and to the end of his career he was capable of sealing up one end.

Worrell's great achievement for West Indies, and for cricket generally, was as a captain to weld together all the diverse elements that went together to make up West Indian cricket, and to discipline his teams into giving all they had got at the right moment. He was the first black player to become regular captain of West Indies, and in 1960–61 he took the side to Australia to play the most exciting series ever, including the only tied Test, at Brisbane. The team, their exciting method of play, and their dedication, rekindled public interest in cricket to such an extent in Australia that the Worrell Trophy was established to be the "Ashes" between the two teams. His captaincy was outstanding – sharp in tactical perception, astute in attack and defence (in all the tension of the last over of the tied Test, he remembered to tell Wes Hall "Whatever you do, don't bowl a no-ball") quietly-spoken, almost exaggeratedly calm, he held his team steady in one crisis after another. When he retired from the game, he became Warden at the University of West Indies, and a Jamaican senator. In the New Year Honours list of 1964 he was knighted (an honour that in future years was to fall upon his successor, Garfield Sobers). On March 13, 1967, he died tragically of leukaemia. He was the man who nursed West Indian cricket to its coming-of-age, with intelligence, dignity and high character.

Among the fine cricketers he had under his command were the most famous fast bowling pair between Miller and Lindwall and Lillee and Thomson –Wesley Hall and Charlie Griffith; and, of course, the finest

The hook — the most exciting, and the most dangerous stroke in cricket.

above left: A. C. MacLaren did it in 1900.
above right: Victor Trumper did it in 1910.

So did Greg Chappell, in 1975.

And little Alvin Khallicharran did it, on one leg, when he hit Dennis Lillee for 34 in ten balls at the Oval.

all-rounder the world has ever known, Garfield Sobers.

Memories of Wes Hall are of nothing if not glory, wrote David Frith in *The Fast Man*. A huge, amiable man, he ran a full 30 yards to the wicket from a point somewhere behind extra cover, his semicircular, bounding, accelerating run ("eyes bulging, teeth glinting, crucifix flying") ending in a classical cartwheel action and intimidating follow-through. He took 192 Test wickets in all, and was the first West Indian to do the hat-trick – in India in 1958, in a series in which he was taken as third bowler and finished with 30 Test wickets. He figured prominently in some of the most exciting Test matches ever played, including the pulsating one at Lords in 1963, when he broke Cowdrey's forearm and bowled the final over, his 40th of the innings, in the match which produced two of the most memorable *batting* performances of all time.

First was Ted Dexter's, who in England's first innings hit 70 off 74 balls, noble, disdainful, furious in turn. At the start, Griffith and Hall, in the words of Ian Wooldridge, "like two huge hired assassins, seemed set for a bloodbath". Reaching his 50 by smashing Griffith through the covers, Dexter's bat "flashed like a scimitar and the crack was like a British rifle sending death down into some deep echoing gorge along the North-West Frontier."

Later, in the second innings, when England needed 234 to pull off a win as unlikely as it would have been heroic, Brian Close waded down the wicket yards before the ball was released, swinging mightily, regardless of personal danger, to hit 70 before he was caught at the wicket. His body was covered in stitch marks and bruises before he had finished. The climax came with David Allen, the Number 10, at the striker's end and Colin Cowdrey, left arm in plaster, at the bowler's end, and Hall with two deliveries to go. Allen held out for the draw, which pleased everybody.

Hall's personality was such that not even the batsmen he bombarded could take exception to him; Colin McDonald, of Australia, whom Hall rated as his most courageous opponent, took a horrible battering in the 1960–61 series and at the end of it all presented Hall with his sweater. Hall even "eased the throttle" against younger batsmen; Doug Walters, making his Sheffield Shield debut, received not one bouncer from Hall, playing for Queensland, although Wally Grout, Hall's own wicketkeeper, was not so lucky, having his jaw smashed by a wild delivery down the leg side.

Charlie Griffith, as explosive and often just as fast at the other end, made a formidable ally. He brought his large frame to the wicket at a fairly leisurely trot, and hurled the ball over with a low trajectory, the ball travelling at great speed and skimming towards the line of the

Garfield Sobers, bowling fast – he would open the bowling, switch to orthodox left arm spin or "chinamen" as the wicket and the occasion demanded.

131

batsman, making it difficult for him to sway away from the (many) short deliveries. At the height of his power, many observers, especially those batsmen who had to play against him, were firmly of the opinion that he threw his faster ball, but in fact he was only ever no-balled for throwing by two umpires. The first time was after the Indian captain Nari Contractor had ducked into a bumper and received a blow on the back of the head which fractured his skull; the second by Arthur Fagg at Old Trafford during the 1966 West Indian match against Lancashire. (For many hours Contractor's life was in danger, and Frank Worrell was one of those who gave blood for him.)

Sir Garfield Sobers is acknowledged to have been the finest all-rounder in the history of the game. At the height of his powers it was said that he was worth three men to any team he played in; if not four for his marvellous close-to-the-wicket fielding. He could bowl fast-medium left-arm, bowling with lithe economy over the wicket and slanting the ball across the right-hand batsman and, when he wished, curling it back at him with a monstrous in-swinger. He could then switch to bowling orthodox left-arm slow-medium after the style of Verity, with chinamen and googlies thrown in for good measure. And as a batsman he was without equal in his time. In his twenty-year career, from 1954 to 1974, he amassed more records than he could ever be bothered to count, among them the highest individual Test score (365), scored the highest individual number of Test runs (8032), appeared in 93 Tests, more than any other cricketer except Cowdrey, and captained West Indies 39 times; and for good measure is the only batsman to have hit six sixes off a six-ball over in first-class cricket. He played for Barbados for 21 seasons, in English League cricket for eight, for South Australia in the Sheffield Shield for three, and Nottinghamshire, who he captained, for seven. John Arlott, in a tribute to him at the close of his career, after he had been knighted in the 1975 Honours List, wrote: "Everything he did was marked by a natural grace, apparent at first sight. As he walked out to bat, six feet tall, lithe but with adequately wide shoulders, he moved with strides which, even when he was hurrying, had an air of laziness, the hip joints rippling like those of a great cat. He was, it seems, born with basic orthodoxy in batting; the fundamental reason for his high scoring lay in the correctness of defence. Once he had established (and he did not always settle in quickly) his sharp eye, early assessment, and inborn gift of timing, enabled him to play almost any stroke. Neither a back-foot nor a front-foot player, he was either as the ball and conditions demanded. When he stepped out and drove it was with a full flow of the bat and a complete followthrough in the classical manner. When he could not get to the pitch of the ball he would go back, wait – as it sometimes seemed –

132

impossibly long – until he identified it and then, at the slightest opportunity, with an explosive whip of the wrists hit it with immense power. His quick reactions and natural ability linked with his attacking instincts made him a brilliant improvisor of strokes. When he was on the kill it was all but impossible to bowl to him – and he was one of the most thrilling of all batsmen to watch."

The stroke I remember him for most was the cover-drive. He would go forward to apparently impossibly short balls to drive. Then he would wait, leaning over into the line, and stroke the ball, on the up, with exquisite timing, to the boundary. It nearly always went to the boundary, for Sobers seemed to have the liaison between wrist and eye, and the speed of reaction, seemingly to look up while the ball was in the air from the bowler's arm, and then direct the shot straight, wide, square or behind square, according to position of the fieldsmen. And always along the ground.

Rohan Kanhai and Clive Lloyd, different in styles as chalk and cheese, both had this inherited ability to drive "on the up". But Kanhai will be remembered more for his flashing square-cut and amazing sweeping, and Lloyd, until the cares of captaincy seemed to have dulled his personal powers somewhat, for the classic left-hander's flick, taking the ball off the leg stump and lifting it, without apparent effort, over long leg's head into the crowd. Gordon Greenidge, quite capable of hitting the first ball of a Test match for six, Roy Fredericks and Alvin Kallicharran, a pint-sized bundle of energy, with a love of hooking fast bowling, are all exciting batsmen in their own right, but the current West Indies team is most distinguished for one batsman, in the lordly classical vein, and yet another pack of extremely fast bowlers, who laid England on the rack in the 1976 series.

The batsman is Vivian Richards, since Sobers and Norman O'Neill, the most avaricious run-gatherer of them all. He is 5ft 9in., well-built, with an upright stance, a withering square-cut and a majestic off- and cover-drive. If he has a weakness, it seems to exist only in his eagerness to get moving at the wicket, which makes him liable to touch an outswinger early on in his innings. Once over that, however, he is as nearly impossible to bowl to as Sobers, as the toiling England bowlers found in 1976. Indeed that year has been his best so far, but as he is only 26 at the time of writing, there are plenty of seasons left in which he must certainly garner more records.

In the first eight months of that year, in 11 Test matches, Richards accumulated 1710 runs with the style and consistency of a great player. His sequence started with 44, 2, 30, 101, 50 and 98 against the lethal Lillee-Thomson combination in the last 3 games of West Indies' disastrous, losing tour of Australia. It continued in the Caribbean, with

Vivian Richards – the greatest batsman of the late 'seventies.

134

scores of 142, 130, 20 run out, 177, 23 and 64, against India and the best spinners in the current game; and in the beautiful English summer of '76, he helped himself to 829 runs in 7 innings, including scores of 291, 232 and 135. His aggregate in Tests in England was the highest by any West Indian in a single series, and yet he missed one Test through illness.

As *Wisden* said, in making him one of its traditional Five Cricketers of the Year, if he fails to make another run in Test cricket his performances in this single year will always be a source of conversation for the enthusiasts and inspiration to young batsmen.

The trio of fast bowlers, Andy Roberts, Michael Holding and Wayne Daniel, form currently the most formidable attack of any international team in the world. Roberts was the first to come to the fore. He was sent from Antigua with Vivian Richards to Alf Gover's cricket school, and from there joined Hampshire. In his first full season he took 119 wickets at an average 13.62, heading the English first-class averages. As the West Indies spearhead, he maintained that form, heading the West Indies averages in the losing tour to Australia; but, mentally and physically tired, he left the destruction of India to another newcomer, Michael Holding, in the home series that followed. Refreshed, he returned to the fray against England in the summer of 1976, and with Holding proceeded to take the England batsmen apart. Each took 28 wickets in the series.

He has a loping, straight run-up and one of those explosive delivery strides pulling the ball down from his full height and using his back as the fulcrum of the catapult. He uses the bouncer, but much more sparingly than his comrades-in-arms. Most batsmen who have faced them both say that he is usually as fast as Lillee, but can be as quick as Thomson at his quickest when he lets the ball go.

In contrast, Michael Holding has the smoothest run-up of all, a graceful rhythmic action which culminates in a ball of frightening speed. His approach must be very similar to that of Ted McDonald, the Australian speedster of the 'twenties. His arms whirl towards the end, and his delivery is without any obvious explosion of effort, but the ball travels at a ferocious speed. In the Indian tour of West Indies, Holding's short-pitched bowling had forced an amazing capitulation by the Indian captain, Bedi. With two of his leading batsmen retired hurt in the first innings, he declared at 306 for 6, feeling that his last three batsmen faced serious injury. In the second innings the Indian innings terminated with only 5 wickets down, at 97, leaving West Indies 13 runs to win. In India's first innings Gaekwad (81) was hit stunningly on the left ear and Viswanath (8) had a finger broken, both by Holding. Patel (14) needed stitches to a facial cut after being hit by Holder. Bedi himself and Chandrasekhar were both injured in the field.

To Holding and Roberts and Holder (no mean performer himself) was added Daniel, and the attack, which brought about the slowest over rate ever in Tests (often down to 12 overs in the hour), was a fearsome one to face. At Trent Bridge in 1976, West Indies were held at bay by last-ditch innings by the veterans, Edrich, Close and Steele and the match at Lord's was drawn, honourably enough. But at Manchester Roberts took 9 and Holding 7 English wickets, and West Indies won by 425 runs. They established a winning lead by taking the fourth Test at Leeds by 55 runs, and then, at The Oval, Holding produced a most inspired piece of fast bowling to beat England almost single-handed. After Richards had hit 291 to take the match out of England's grasp, Holding captured 8 for 92 in the first innings and 6 for 57, hitting the stumps no fewer than nine times. It was a supreme exhibition of pace and accuracy on the traditionally dead Oval pitch. Only Dennis Amiss, with 203, faced him with any confidence – and Holding bowled hardly a single bumper.

Wayne Daniel is built like a tank, and like one he ploughs his way to the wicket, taking two gigantic strides to deliver the ball. He is often inaccurate, but his better balls are often unplayable. He makes a formidable number three in the West Indian attack, and in 1977 he was one of the main factors in Middlesex's retaining at least a share of the County Championship.

In all, West Indies seem well equipped for the future.

The contribution of South African cricketers through the years reached its peak in 1966–67 when for the first time Australia lost a Test series to them – by three matches to one, and again in 1969–70, when Bill Lawry's side were thoroughly drubbed, all four matches going convincingly to the South Africans. Since then, however, for political reasons, South African cricket, along with most other sports, has been effectively isolated from the rest of the world, and only in the exploits of a few outstanding players who have to make their careers overseas can the world estimate South African standards of today.

Immediately after the war, the South African banner was carried by A. D. Nourse, Jr, who dominated the country's batting for most of his career and scored nine hundreds for his country. He was a solid, all-round batsman with all the strokes, and he once made 208 against England with a broken thumb, a feat of courage and endurance hard to match. With him were Bruce Mitchell and Alan Melville, the latter captain of South Africa in the years immediately before and after the war.

During the mid-fifties there was little Jackie McGlew (christened by the Press McGlue after taking 545 minutes to reach 100 against

136

Australia at Durban in 1957–58). Strangely, the little man with the cast-iron defence and the master of the forward prod, could also score well, and in fact he stands higher in the statistical merit table, with 2440 runs at an average of 42.06, than the two golden boys of the era, Roy McLean and Johnny Waite, the wicketkeeper.

McLean was a draw wherever he played. Dark, handsome and freehitting, he knew of only one delight, which was to belt the cover off the ball; but he had a good defence too, and his restless, happy-go-lucky approach brought him five Test centuries, three against England. His cover-driving was in a class of its own. Waite, who still stands high in the international wicketkeeping table, was tall for a 'keeper, but he caught 124 and stumped 17 batsmen in Tests; and his 2405 runs in international cricket were mostly made with handsome, classical strokes on the off side, especially the cut.

Strangely, although South Africa has always had a reasonable supply of good fast bowlers, only J. J. Kotze, in the early part of the century, and R. J. Crisp, from the 'thirties, really stand out; and it was not until the mid and late 'fifties, when Neil Adcock and Peter Heine were brought together, that South Africa had a pace attack worth the name. They were a fierce, combative partnership, though Adcock was by far the better and more effective bowler, with a high, loose-limbed action, and considerable pace. He took 104 wickets in his 26 Tests. Heine's value was more nuisance, or rather intimidation. He was one of the most genuinely belligerent bowlers of the time, more so even than Freddie Trueman. Jim Laker records that Heine appeared really amused if he hit someone, and was infuriated by Trevor Bailey's dour defensive batting. "I want to hit you, Bailey, I want to hit you over the heart," he snarled once, although Bailey, I am sure, only prodded all the more dourly.

As they faded, their place was taken by Peter Pollock, the elder of two cricketing prodigies, and all-rounder Eddie Barlow, the burly, genial competitor who now bowls leg- and off-spin for Derbyshire, but at that time bowled fast-medium back-up to Pollock. Pollock, tall and fair-haired, was a maddening bowler to a nervous batsman, for he took a very long, time-consuming run-up, the ball held low by his side and his knees coming up high. With his height, he could make the ball rear from just short of a length. In the 1969–70 series against Australia he took 15 wickets (average 17.20) but the real damage was done at the other end by a new fireball, Mike Procter. Procter's deeds for Gloucestershire over the past few years have made of him a legend to rival that of the great Doctor himself. In 1966–67 he took 7 Australian wickets on his debut, and 6 in the next. In 1970 he was undoubtedly the fastest bowler in the world (until "Thommo" and Roberts appeared he prob-

Two views of how not to bowl and succeed in spite of it. Mike Procter, of South Africa, defying all the known laws of physics to bowl (after a marathon run) fast off the back foot and follow-though like a sack of coal.

138

ably maintained that position) and he took 26 wickets at an average of a mere 13.57.

Procter runs from so far back that on small grounds he has to kick off from the sightscreen. He can be maddeningly slow on the walk-back to his mark, but once he is launched on his run he goes absolutely flat out, and one is reminded that he once did the 100 yards in evens. He is almost unique in that he bowls off the "wrong" foot, with a double-circular action of the arms, bringing the right arm over at the same time that the right leg is going forward. With this disconcerting action (disconcerting, that is to say, to a batsman used to the normal right-hander's build-up – by the Procter method the ball leaves the hand that much sooner than expected, and can ruin the rhythm of the shot) he can make the ball dip in alarmingly or run away from the bat at will. And as he is at his best an imperious right-hand batsman, there are few who would challenge the claim that since Sobers retired, Procter has been the world's outstanding all-rounder.

Mention Colin Bland, and the reaction from any cricket-lover is "fielding". His exploits in England in 1965 gained him world renown. He ran out Barrington and Jim Parks on the same afternoon at Lord's, and at Canterbury gave (at Colin Cowdrey's insistent request, because the modest Bland would never have so thrust himself forward) a most amazing display of fielding for the photographers. Three stumps were set up in front of a net and then someone got a box of six balls and rolled them out, one by one, to Bland, about ten yards to his right and then ten yards to his left, at cover-point distance, about 25 yards away. Bland never stopped moving. He swooped on them in turn and in one flowing movement threw them on the run. With his first throw he knocked the stumps sideways; with the next two he missed, by a whisker; with his fourth throw he knocked two stumps out of the ground and with his fifth he laid the remaining one flat. He was cheered to the echo by about 2000 lucky spectators, just as he had been when he ran out Parks by throwing the ball through the batsman's legs, under his body, as he raced for home. Bland is the only man who could add thousands to any gate at a cricket match by his fielding alone.

I have three memories of Bland. First, I remember him and his father on the Queen's Club at Bulawayo when he was a mere lad, before the 1956–57 MCC tour of South Afirca. The father would throw out the balls, for hours on end, while his son picked them up, always on the run, and returned them to a single stump. The second is when he was an international star, seeing him get fit for the cricketing season. He was running "on the spot" in a shower cubicle off a changing room we were using for a hockey match. He was still running as we went out to knock up for the match; still running at half-time when we ducked in

Colin Bland – probably the best fieldsman the world's ever seen.

to check up; and still running on the same spot when we came off the field after the match, the walls and floor of the shower soaked with his sweat. And the third is of keeping wicket behind Bland while he scored 215 in a Mashonaland first league match. The ball passed the bat four times that day as Bland's fours and sixes peppered the sightscreen. The fourth time was when, past 200, he mishit a gentle little lob over his head in my direction. I was so mesmerised by this time that I stood, rooted to the spot, and watched it fall to ground a yard in front of me.

South Africa has always been blessed with a fine supply of spin bowlers. In the early days it was all leg-break and googly, which the South Africans borrowed from the great Bosanquet and almost re-patented as their own invention. But since the Second World War the off-spinner has predominated through Lindsay Tuckett, Athol Rowan and, the best of them all, Hugh Tayfield. Tayfield stands way out on his own at the head of South African bowling records, with 170 wickets in Tests.

Fourteen times he took 5 wickets in an innings. He was most naggingly accurate, and would take his wickets on good pitches as well as bad. Tayfield was not so much a great *spinner* as a great *bowler*. In fact he rarely spun the ball hard at all. He had a curious action. Bowling over the wicket, he placed his front (left) foot across immediately in front of the stumps, swivelling on the ball of his foot and bringing his arm down over the stumps or even farther to leg. His line of attack was most unusual, a straight ball pitching on middle stump would hit off stump, and therefore the usual rules of playing an off-spinner to leg with the spin did not apply. His field was set with only four on the leg side and two of those in catching positions – very often two silly mid-ons, one saving the single at square leg and the fourth halfway to the boundary behind the silly mid-ons. After Tayfield bowled he would come to a dead stop poised as another close fielder in front of the wicket. One slip and four men in the covers would complete his field, with sometimes a very deep mid-off. It was all very inhibiting to the batsman, who would as often as not get himself out hitting across the line in sheer frustration.

Finally, South African cricket has produced two very great batsmen indeed, though much of their talent has been wasted in the arid desert of apartheid and politics. Graeme Pollock and Barry Richards, left- and right-hand respectively, have been among the freest-scoring batsmen. Pollock, tall, graceful, the youngest South African ever to score a double-century, is capable, like Bradman, of demolishing any attack with fluency and power; Richards, everyone who has seen him bat agrees, was the most graceful player in the first-class English game before he left the county scene during the 1978 season. They both have a fault; in Richards it is that it is all too easy for him, and he is inclined (as Hammond sometimes did in the 'thirties) to get himself out through sheer boredom after rounding the century mark; with Pollock, it is his Compton-like ability to run his partners out. His captain, Ali Bacher, used to say that it was because the partner was so mesmerised by the brilliance of Pollock's strokes that he wouldn't wake up until Pollock was three-quarters of the way down the wicket yelling "Come on!"

As I write, another young South African star is rising. He is left-hand batsman Kepler Wessels, and he has already made a startling beginning to his first-class career, with Sussex, though he is not yet 21. His batting has an air of inevitability and composure remarkable in one so young; indeed he seems surprised not to make a hundred every time he goes in to bat. It's the sort of attitude and spirit that Tony Greig, the former Sussex and England captain, regards as a cricketer's main asset.

*   *   *   *   *

Sarfraz Nawaz – a fast bowler in direct line of descent from F. R. Spofforth.

Since the days of Ranjitsinhji, the Indian sub-continent has brought charm and Oriental magic to the more strictly Anglo-Saxon merits of world cricket. After Ranji and his nephew Duleepsinhji, the Nawabs of Pataudi, father and son (who is now Mansur Ali Khan) graced the cricket field in their turn.

In recent years, India has been better known for her classic spin bowlers, like Bishan Bedi, certainly the best left-arm spinner of the 'seventies, and Chandrasekhar, now past his best, but a leg-spinner and googly bowler with the pace and the class of Doug Wright.

Vinoo Mankad, bowling left-arm slows the batting right-handed somewhat faster, is one of the few men to have hit over 2000 Test runs and taken more than 100 Test wickets. He was a powerful all-round-the-wicket player. At Madras, in 1955, he and Pankaj Roy created the Test record for the first wicket partnership, hitting 413 against New Zealand. Roy, incidentally, hit 140 in his first Test against England, but then, in 1952, had the unfortunate experience of making five ducks in seven innings in a Test series, also against England.

Vijay Manjrekar, a stylish batsman noted for his sound defence, totalled over 3000 runs for India in Tests, second only to Pahlan ("Polly") Umrigar, who hit twelve hundreds in his 3631 runs. He was the most confident of batsmen, making his runs on all types of wickets.

Bedi, who delights his followers, and there are many all over the world, by bowling in a different coloured turban each day, holds the Indian record for Test bowling, with 246 wickets, followed by Chandrasekhar (222), Prasanna (187), Mankad (162), Gupte (149), and Venkataraghavan (113). It is remarkable that all these bowlers are spinners; and it is also remarkable that they work their eastern magic best on the dry and dusty wickets of their home country.

When the sub-continent was partitioned, Pakistan was left with few first-class cricketers. But subsequently the newest full member of the International Cricket Conference has proved a formidable opponent for the strongest teams.

By far their most outstanding batsman has been Hanif Mohammad, who holds more records than is good for any one man: the highest score ever made by an individual in first-class cricket – 499; the longest innings – 337 in 970 minutes, at Bridgetown in 1957–58, when he batted three days to save the match against West Indies; and the slowest 20 – that took him 195 minutes. This was the little man who, they said when he went into his country's team, was too small and frail to hit the ball to the boundary – he had 64 fours in his 499. His brother Mushtaq, who has just parted company after ten years with Northamptonshire, was another such, except that he added rolypoly leg-spin to his exciting batting; and yet another brother, Sadiq, opens the batting for Gloucestershire.

For pure style, though, Majid Khan, who has recently quit Glamorgan, has looked the best of them all. Upright, calm and yet a quite ruthless batsman after the manner of Greg Chappell when he is in full flow, Majid is in a class by himself.

And finally, three characters from New Zealand. Martin Donnelly and Bert Sutcliffe vie with each other for the position as the most polished batsman, both left-handers, and both with impeccable style. Sutcliffe goes into the record books more, as Donnelly's career was spent mainly in England. Sutcliffe was perhaps the most technically correct batsman his country has ever produced, with a fine record

John Reid's style and character lifted him above such New Zealand stars as Martin Donnelly and Bert Sutcliffe.

against much stronger teams. Because of that, his later career was over-shadowed by injuries.

But John Reid, of all cricketers, stands in a class of his own in New Zealand cricket. For most of the time he played, and for all of the time he captained New Zealand, it needed all his optimism and considerable strength of character to keep his country's head above water. He was one of the most powerful men ever to play cricket, and he hit the ball like a thunderbolt. In 58 Tests he scored 3431 runs and took 85 wickets; and the peak of his career came in 1962, when he took New Zealand to South Africa. Not only did New Zealand win two of the Tests (their first ever victories against South Africa) but his own performances were astonishing. He not only headed the batting in the Test tables, but averaged *twice* as many as the next man. His tour aggregate was just under 2000 runs, while Dowling's, the next man's, was 715. His total was the highest ever made by a tourist in South Africa, more than Compton or May. Not only did Reid score seven hundreds, but he took 22 catches close to the wicket, and took 11 wickets in the series at lower cost than anyone else.

And in the next season, against England at home, he scored 100 out of his side's total of 159 when Trueman was on the rampage. He was a giant among mere mortals, a splendid back-foot batsman, a versatile fast-medium bowler, and a captain for all seasons. And when he was eighteen, he had to give up rugby, because rheumatic fever had left him, of all things, with a weak heart!

There are wicketkeepers and wicketkeepers, and longstops with gloves on. With all due respect to the marvellous athleticism of Alan Knott and Rodney Marsh, to their enthusiasm and combative personalities, I don't think either England or Australia have fielded a genuine wicketkeeper of class and *style* since the days of Godfrey Evans and Gil Langley respectively; and the one benefit of the whole Packer affair is that it has given a genuinely stylish 'keeper in Bob Taylor the chance to show what he can do in the highest company. In addition, with a youngster called Paul Downton getting his chance with an England touring side, there seems some indication that once again we shall be watching really high-class wicketkeeping, as opposed to mere stopping, for the next decade or so.

I was fortunate enough to receive a fortnight's concentrated coaching at the hands of one of the finest wicketkeepers never to have played for England, Tommy Wade of Essex. Not, I may add hastily, that it made a great deal of difference to my own average performances, but it made me highly critical of wicketkeeping styles and gave me some insight at least into the special pressures to which 'keepers are subjected. To take two very simple examples. A first-class wicketkeeper will never (repeat never) take a ball with his gloved fingers pointing towards its flight; always vertically downwards, below the waist if possible; or vertically upwards if higher near the body. To try to catch the ball with the fingers pointing towards the flight of the ball leads to broken fingers and broken careers. And again, observe the "class" 'keeper carefully. He will never go down behind the stumps on the balls of his feet, as if he is going to leap straight from the squat position towards the flight of the ball. He bends his knees and goes down into the position *with his feet flat on the ground.* Try it yourself and see why. If you crouch down on the soles of your feet, you will find every muscle through the foot, ankle, calf and thigh tense and stretched. Try it up, down, up, down, through an innings lasting two days and more, as is common in Test matches, and you'll be a mass of cramps.

The really great wicketkeepers over the years have been distinguished from the merely average in a number of ways. First, their ability (and courage) to be able to "stand up to" – that is, to be close behind the stumps to – bowling up to and including fast-medium. Second, their ability to perform their various tasks neatly and without fuss. Third, their ability to *make the fielding look good.* And fourth, to "take" on the leg side.

How many modern wicketkeepers does one watch covering up their deficiencies in one or more areas? The loud and vociferous appeal, for example, designed to persuade the umpire by intimidation rather than reason. Or running twenty yards to receive a loosely-thrown-in ball and glaring, arms akimbo, at the fieldsman?

It is possible, I suppose, to blame the fall-off in the standard of wicketkeeping to the modern preponderance of "seam" bowling; to the dearth of "class" spinners or the cautiousness of modern batsmen. I believe the responsibility lies in the percentage attitude – the one which says that you may miss a few stumping chances by not "standing up" but you give away fewer extras in the form of byes, and you're more likely to take catches standing back than immediately behind the stumps.

The figures tell the story. Three times in his career Les Ames, the Kent and England all-rounder, took 100 wickets or more as follows:

Year	Ct	St	Total
1932	36	64	100
1929	79	48	127
1928	69	52	121

The last time the feat was performed was in 1964 by Roy Booth of Worcestershire, with 91 catches and 9 stumpings. In 1967 Alan Knott, England's top 'keeper, returned 35 catches and 3 stumpings.

146

Kent have made something of a tradition of providing England's wicketkeepers. Alan Knott, with his mannerisms, his perpetual restless isometrics, and his imp's grin (which is as much a grin as it is the nervously stretched grimace of the thoroughbred under pressure) has been the incumbent until recently; indeed, his increasingly formidable batting gives him the claim to be a stylist in both disciplines. He is amazingly athletic, throwing himself yards to turn leg-glances into catching chances; only close up behind the stumps does he fail to match the giants of the past.

Of these, Godfrey Evans has been the undoubted master since the Second World War. Short, with forearms equipped with the muscles of the wrestler, Evans had the perky self-assurance of the London sparrow. He was forever restless, like Knott, forever on the move, but in his "business" he was the neatest and fastest of them all. When I last saw him play, white-haired, red-faced and well into the mid-fifties, he was still taking the ball instinctively, his hands a blur of speed over the leg stump, legs across, in perfect position for the stumping. He had the ability to inspire a fielding side merely with his presence, his enthusiasm, and his sheer expertise. He would stand up to England's fastest bowler of his day, Alec Bedser, even on wet wickets. He would stop the ball on his bare forearm, and never wince nor pause to rub the injured spot. John Arlott called him the most unquenchable man in all cricket. "He will greet the batsman at the crease with a wink, pull his leg, stump him with an appeal paralysing in its speed and sharpness, commiserate with him, replace the bails, and be waiting impatiently for the next man in – all within seconds. Never, surely, as a cricketer so boiling over with vitality or so prodigal with energy. ... He has the fastest and cleanest hands for the ball that the mind of a cricketer can imagine, and he tries for everything."

Memorable though the feats of Knott and Evans may have been, you could write their records, and those of the other famous Kent wicketkeepers (like Huish and Hubble) on the back of one of Leslie Ames's gloves. Ames was the finest wicketkeeper-batsman England has ever produced, scoring a grand total of over 37,000 runs, including 102 centuries, eight of them in Tests. He hit 1000 runs in a season seventeen times, including over 3000 in 1933. It was said, when Freeman bowled and Ames kept wicket for Kent, it was nothing less than a campaign of intimidation.

Before Ames, England's fortunes behind the wicket were shared between two apparently indestructible cricketers, Herbert Strudwick and George Duckworth. Strudwick, the holder of the record number of wickets taken by a keeper (1493) until surpassed by Middlesex's John Murray with 1527, was a neat, imperturbable cricketer to whom the

There are wicketkeepers and longstops with gloves on. . . .

above: Bert Oldfield. "It's good to get 'em."
below: Godfrey Evans. "Could inspire any team."

Alan Knott. "A bundle of nerves, fanaticism and genius."

Bob Taylor. "Quietly, probably the best of the lot . . ."

greatest compliment would have been that you didn't even notice he was playing. This was in direct line from "Dick" Lilley, whose unflashy swiftness and undoubtedly deep knowledge of the game endeared him to all. He kept the England position his own from 1896 to 1909, and he was Strudwick's hero. At the start of his career he "stood up" even to the fastest, like Tom Richardson or Walter Brearley; until W. G. Grace himself advised: "Why stay there and be *killed*?" C. B. Fry, who found it difficult to make a preference between him and one or two other well-known 'keepers of the times, said: "Like all first-rate wicketkeepers, he is quiet and simple behind the sticks, and does not snatch at the balls. His catching and stumping area, of course of the finest description, and he is a marvel at taking wide, inaccurate returns from the fieldsmen; he seems to stretch out a couple of yards from the wicket, gather the ball, and sweep it in, all in one action."

His main rival was Gregor MacGregor of Middlesex, who had been together with Sam Woods at Cambridge. The two knew each other's styles intimately, and MacGregor stood close up to Woods when he was at his fastest. He would place his hands wide open in the spot where he thought the ball should be bowled, and Sam Woods would send the ball straight into them. "As the position of the wicketkeeper is admirably adapted for inspecting very closely what a batsman is doing," said C. B. Fry, "and as Mr MacGregor is extremely quick at picking out the weak point in a man's game, it can readily be understood that his suggestive actions behind the wicket were very valuable to the bowler."

Suggestive gestures, indeed. Tell that to Rodney Marsh.

The great-grand-daddy of Australian 'keepers was undoubtedly a marvellous cricketer called John McCarthy Blackham, who stood up to the fireballs of Spofforth in the first Test in 1877, kept wicket for Australia for twenty years, and captained his country to boot. George Giffen called him "The Prince of Wicketkeepers".

"During the whole of his first-class career he was peerless as a wicketkeeper. One could not help admiring him as he stood behind the stumps at a critical period in the game. With eyes as keen as a hawk, and regardless of knocks, he would take the fastest bowling with marvellous dexterity, and woe betide the batsman who even so much as lifted the heel of his back foot as he played forward and missed the ball."

In 1884, when the Australian XI defeated the Gentlemen of England by 46 runs, Blackham *stumped* the last three batsmen. He was a grand judge of the game and few could more quickly detect a weakness in a batsman; but he made a poor captain because of his nerves; and in fact during one three-months series, Blackham lost a stone in weight,

150

which he attributed himself to worry and anxiety.

If Blackham established an Australian wicketkeeping style, it was William Albert "Bert" Oldfield who made himself into a legend. Small, quiet, neat and unbelievably quick with his hands, he took the thunderbolts of Gregory and McDonald with nonchalant ease. Writing in *Wisden*, Rowland Ryder described how in the fourth Test match of Gillingan's exciting tour to Australia in 1924–25, Oldfield really established himself as wicketkeeper supreme. In England's first and only innings, with reflexes of astonishing speed, he stumped Hobbs, Woolley, Chapman and Whysall. The *pièce de résistance* was the dismissal of Hobbs, when Jack Ryder sent down an unexpectedly fast delivery that rose cap high. Hobbs, in avoiding the ball, moved momentarily out of his crease, and Oldfield, in the meantime, took the ball in front of his nose and flicked the bail off. In his 54 Tests for Australia, Oldfield "bagged" 130 victims – 52 of them stumped. Admittedly, he had Mailey, Grimmett and O'Reilly doing most of the bowling. Charlie Macartney used to say that you didn't know he was there until he'd got you out – his appeal was quiet, almost apologetic – and J. H. Fingleton said that if he congratulated Oldfield on a particularly smart piece of stumping, the only reply would be an embarrassed, "It's nice to get them, isn't it?"

Both Wally Grout (187) and Rodney Marsh (198) have taken more wickets in Test matches for Australia; but these days the dearth of the genuine spinner and the concentration on high-speed bowling has led to the disappearance of one of the finest sights of cricket – the flashing stumping off the quick bowlers that used to turn a match in the twinkling of an eye. Of Knott's 252 Test wickets, only 19 have been stumped; of Marsh's 198 – only 8 stumped. But, as these things have always gone in waves, perhaps the time is now returning when we shall be able to appreciate, once again, true style behind the stumps. It's nice to think so, isn't it?

7

Plenty of Hope

To return to the start, the definition of "style". You will have gathered that my belief where cricket is concerned is that style must produce results, both for player and spectator. To be stylish is not necessarily to have style, and in fact in the curious shades of meaning the English language develops, the adjective stylish sometimes conveys merely that the person concerned pretends to style, rather than possesses it. The amiable Bannister, who played for Tillingfold in Hugh de Selincourt's fictional *Cricket Match*, was one such. He took guard immaculately, drawing out his mark with the toe of his boot, examining the field-setting minutely, and then settling to a relaxed and meaningful stance. The bowler, who knew his man, delivered a slow, straight ball on a good length. Bannister played forward perfectly, his bat next to his pad, nicely balanced and with pleasing style. The ball carried straight through, not deviating an inch, and gently bowled him.

The Bannisters of this world have no place in this book, although without doubt they occur in cricket as in all walks of life. But on looking back, I wonder if I have managed to establish my thesis. Is there a pedigree running from Grace, through MacLaren and Hobbs to Hammond and Peter May; from Bradman to Neil Harvey; from Jessop and Trumper through Macartney and McCabe to Denis Compton; from Shaw and Spofforth, through Jones, Gregory and Larwood to Tyson, Statham, Lindwall and Lillee? Where would you fit Thomson? Who ever produced strokes as magical as Woolley's, or garnered runs with the dedication of a Lawry? Was Bosanquet as good a bowler as O'Reilly?

The best cricket cameraman in television, George Richardson, who would film every ball of an entire Test match in order to place one minute of the day's play on the news screen, used to say: "The moment you think you've got cricket taped, it gets up and hits you." On reflection, I think that's what cricket's done to me. The true fascination of the game lies not in its predictability, but in its infinite variety.

But it's been fun finding out.

152

Indian guile in the form of Bishan Bedi. Beautiful orthodox left-arm spinner.

Acknowledgments

The author's thanks and acknowledgments are due to many authors and publishers for use of their material; to the Library at Lord's for their assistance; and to Miss Pamela Spofforth, grand-daughter of F. R. Spofforth, for setting me forth on this quest with both information and encouragement.

Bailey, Trevor, *The Greatest of my Time*, Eyre and Spottiswoode.

Batchelor, Denzil, (editor), *The Great Cricketers*, Eyre and Spottiswoode.

Bedser, Alec, *Bowling*, Hodder and Stoughton.

Bettesworth, W. A., *Chats on the Cricket Field*, Merritt and Hatcher.

Cardus, Neville, *Cricket Discourse*, Harrap.

Cardus, Neville, *Days in the Sun*, Jonathan Cape and Rupert Hart-Davis.

Cowdrey, Colin, *M.C.C.*, Hodder and Stoughton.

Cowdrey, Colin, *Tackle Cricket This Way*, Stanley Paul.

Dexter, E. R., *Ted Dexter's Cricket Book*, Arthur Barker.

Fingleton, Jack, *Brightly Fades the Don*, Collins Publishers.

Frith, David, *The Fast Men*, Richard Smart Publishing.

Fry, C. B., (editor), *The Book of Cricket*, George Newnes.

Giffen, George, *With Bat and Ball*, Ward, Lock.

Hayter, Reg, (editor), *Cricket Stars of Today*, Pelham Books.

James, C. L. R., *Beyond a Boundary*, Hutchinson.

Laker, Jim, *Spinning Round the World*, Frederick Muller.

Mailey, Arthur, *Cricket Heroes*, J. M. Dent.

Mailey, Arthur, *10 for 66 and All That*, J. M. Dent.

Moyes, A. G., *The Noblest Game; Australian Bowlers*, George G. Harrap.

Peebles, Ian, *Talking about Cricket*, Museum Press.

Snow, John, *Cricket: How to Become a Champion*, William Luscombe.

Thomson, A. A., *Cricketers of My Times*, Stanley Paul.

Thomson, A. A., *Hutton and Washbrook*, Epworth Press.

Thomson, A. A., *The Great Cricketer*, Robert Hale.

The Cricketer, various editions.
Playfair Cricket Monthly.
Wisden Cricketers' Almanack, various editions.

One stylist of the future. David Gower represents the hopes of all those who are convinced that style and grace have not been lost or submerged in the professional glitter of the Packer circus.

Picture credits

The author and publishers gratefully acknowledge the assistance of David Frith in researching the photographs for this book, Patrick Eagar for his help, and the following for permission to reproduce illustrations:

Central Press Photos Ltd: pp. 74, 76 (right), 78, 91 (right), 94, 102, 105, 122, 140, 148 (bottom).
Patrick Eagar: pp. 7, 47 (right), 85 (bottom), 91 (left), 95, 108 (bottom), 109, 111, 123, 129, 131, 134, 138, 142, 149, 153, 155.
Ken Kelly: p. 29.
The Press Association Ltd: p. 76 (left).
Sport and General: p. 117 (top).

Index

Note: 'p' indicates occasional references to an item on the pages cited.

159